When Have We Walked TOGETHER?

JAMES THORNTON

Rapier
PUBLISHING COMPANY

Unless otherwise noted, Scripture quoted from the NIV, Amplified, KJV, and NASB are from the Comparative Study Bible, revised edition,
Copyright 1999
Zondervan Publishing House
All rights reserved.

All other scriptures quoted are from the
The Hebrew-Greek Key Study Bible, King James Version, Red Letter Edition,
Editors: Spiros Zodhaites & Warren Baker
AMG Publishers, Chattanooga, TN, 1991

Copyright © 2012 by James Thornton

When Have We Walked Together?
978-0-9839483-9-1

Published by
Rapier Publishing Company, LLC
3417 Rainbow Parkway
Rainbow City, Alabama 35906

www.rapierpublishing.com

Library of Congress Control Number: 2012955556

Printed in the United States of America

All rights reserved under International Copyright Law.
Contents and/or cover may not be reproduced in whole or in part
in any form without the consent of the Publisher

Book Design by:
Drew Key (Key Koncept)
Delaney-Designs

Book Layout:
Delaney-Designs

Dedications

I would like to dedicate this book to my wife Nathalee. Thank you for giving me the support that was needed, and for standing with me, and covering me with prayer. To my children, Cynthia, Austell, Mechelle, and James; and my son-in-law Johnny Ray Pruitt. Thank you for your prayers, support, and encouragement.

To my parents, Oscar and Bernice Thornton. My dad was the most incredible man I have ever known. Also, to my brothers and sisters.

To my pastors, mentors, and special gifts, Dr. Hart Ramsey and Mrs. Alethia Ramsey, thank you for the words of encouragement, and the level of teaching I have received at Northview Christian Church, Dothan, Alabama. As a result of your teaching, I have received more revelation and understanding of the things of God. This book is a combination of that revelation and my connection to you and Northview Christian Church.

Acknowledgements

To my publisher, Fannie A. Pierce, Rapier Publishing Company. Thank you for your unbelievable labor of love, dedication, and discipline in bringing everything together. You were ordained by the Lord Jesus for this project.

To the many members of Northview Christian Church (NCC): Elder Pete Pierce Jr., Elder Preston White, Elder Yvette Hogan, Elder Deborah Rivers, Ministers Gerald and Alicia Brown, Minister Brian Evans, Minister Raymond Ramsey, Minister Rosalind Harrison, Deaconess Sallie Daniel, Mrs. Kintenia Harris, Mrs. Cheryl Boatwright, and to the entire NCC family for your support and encouragement.

I would like to express my appreciation to Dr. Hart Ramsey, Dr. Myles Monroe and Dr. Frederick K. C. Price. The integrity and commitment they have demonstrated is invaluable to me.

FOREWORD

Few men understand or perceive life as James Thornton does. His passion for truth and decades of observation has shaped him to be a man of few words and deep conviction. As my Associate Pastor of many years, Dr. Thornton has mastered the art of leading from a supportive role and documenting solid answers to probing questions.

In this book, James Thornton tackles the resilient issue of slanted human relationships, how they came to be, and what may be done in an effort to right a ship that has been wrong for some time. Like an attorney arguing a convincing case, he will capture you with facts and opinions that aren't easily refuted. The honest heart will rejoice in this offering. The biased and bigoted will stand rebuked before God and their consciences.

This is a book for the ages with a topic that cannot be ignored. "When Have We Walked Together" is a call to abandon the status quo and reach for the equality and unity that Jesus prayed for in John 17.

I am proud to introduce you to my friend and colleague of many years. Experience the ministry and heart of Dr. James Thornton.

Dr. Hart Ramsey, Senior Pastor
Northview Christian Church/Safe Harbor
Dothan and Montgomery, Alabama

ABOUT THE BOOK

When Ford Manufacturing Company creates a product, a new automobile, before the product is made known or released for the auto industry and the world to see, it is first put through rigorous tests to see if it meets the standards of the manufacturer. In the process of creating the new automobile, there are many facets to be considered, many questions to be answered, and many problems to be resolved before the unveiling.

Every key department has a say in the final creation: the engineers, the designers, even the financial department. Every factor is weighed, instilled, discussed and looked at before the green light is given. There are many things to consider in the process: the steering wheel, the engine, the miles per gallon on the highway and in the city, its driving capability, and also the smoothness of the drive. And don't forget the luxury packets, the "bells and whistles", which makes the creation appeasing to the buyer.

After the product or creation is completed, it is ready to be unveiled. It's a funny thing after the unveiling, many are called experts about how the car runs, its capabilities, and even how to fix it; however, only the manufacturer of the product, Ford, really knows the true capabilities of its creation. Thus, the manufacturer is, therefore, the only one that can really fix the product when it is not working according to its plans and specifications, because it's his creation. Many will go to other agencies or experts to fix the product when it doesn't operate according to standards; however, to get it to work correctly as created, one must go to the one who created it. Yes, it may cost more, but expertise costs, and the manufacturer knows his product. The manufacturer knows what it needs to run effectively again. After all, Ford was the creator of the creation.

When God (the Manufacturer) created man (the product), He (The Holy Trinity) created man in His own image, and likeness. He designed man to have dominion over the fish of the sea, over the fowl of the air, over the cattle (animals), and all over the earth. In addition, He designed man to have dominion over every creeping thing that creeps upon the earth: worms, spiders, lizards, ants, etc. He blessed His creation and said, "Be fruitful and multiply, and replenish the earth and subdue it" (Genesis 1:26-28).

Throughout the book "When Have We Walked Together," the Lord is depicted as the Manufacturer, and man is depicted as the product. The author, in his infallible wisdom, has used this illustration to allow you to comprehend fully the magnitude of what it means when a manufacturer creates a product. The creation does not tell the creator how it is to operate. The creation, or the product, adheres to the specifications of the creator (manufacturer). God is the Creator of man. Man can establish his own specifications, standards, or rules to abide by; however, all of this is null, even if it appears to be working. It is null because it not operating or functioning in the manner it was created.

The Lord designed us in His image and likeness. He designed us to have the Fruit of His Spirit. The Fruit of the Spirit is love, joy, peace, longsuffering, gentleness, goodness, faith, meekness, and temperance (Galatians 5:22-23), empowered by grace. If the product walks in anything other than this, it is a result of following the desires of his sinful nature. This produces sexual immorality, impure thoughts, eagerness for lustful pleasure, idolatry, participation in demonic activities, hostility, quarreling, jealousy, outbursts of anger, selfish ambition, divisions, the feeling that everyone is wrong except those in your own little group, envy, drunkenness, wild parties, and other kinds of sin (Galatians 5:19-21).

Never before has there been a book such as "When Have We Walked Together," which truthfully depicts the position of man and a country when he and it fail to abide by the specifications of their Creator. It is a book that will make you think, possibly get angry, or even at one point cause denial, shame and regret. It will make you see the reality of the truth, and hopefully that Truth will make you free. In the end, hopefully, it will cause you to change – from darkness to light, to become a better citizen for and to all mankind, but more importantly to become all you were destined to be as the Creator created you to be. After all, Man was created after the image of His Creator.

The Publisher,
Rapier Publishing Company, LLC

TABLE OF CONTENTS

Introduction 17
    The Importance of Unity

Chapter One 21
    Religion— The Product's Solution to Reconnect to the Manufacturer

Chapter Two 29
    Religion and the Authority of the People

Chapter Three 37
    A Nation Divided

Chapter Four 47
    The Heart of the Founding Fathers

Chapter Five 55
    The Constitution…The Potential of a Nation

Chapter Six 63
    The Absence of Truth

Chapter Seven 69
    The Truth Will Make Us Free

Chapter Eight 77
    The Iniquity of a Nation

Chapter Nine 87
    Repentance: A Nation's Challenge

Chapter Ten 97
    The Iniquity of the Church

Chapter Eleven 107
    The Great Commission

Chapter Twelve 115
    One Nation Under— Choose This Day Whom You Will Serve

Chapter Thirteen 121
    The Call For Unity— Can We Walk Together?

Final Thoughts 129

Introduction
The Importance of Unity

Walking together requires unity and a common goal of shared beliefs. It places a demand on all participants to focus on the same objective. In Amos 3:3, the requirement for walking together is very clear, "Do two walk together except they make an appointment and have agreed?" From this we learn that walking together requires agreement from all parties, and the result of that agreement is unity. Everyone is on the same accord.

For unity to exist, within a church, a nation, or between a husband and wife, everyone must see through the same eyes, hear the same voice, speak the same language, and perceive in their hearts the same principles of agreement. The power of agreement is so strong that in Matthew 18:19, the Lords states, "Again, I tell you, if two of you on earth agree (harmonize together, make a symphony together) about whatever [anything and everything] they may ask, it will come to pass and be done for them by My Father in heaven." This promise is available to all that walk together in unity.

Unity has both positive and negative effects. For example, in Genesis 11, the power of unity prevailed in such a way that the product (man) sought to build a city and a tower whose top was to reach the heavens. This unity had a negative effect because the objective of the product was to make a name for themselves without regard for the Manufacturer (God). It was to proclaim their greatness and achievement. As a result of their unity, the Manufacturer came down to see the city and the tower which the product had built. In verse 6 it states, "And the Lord said, behold, they are one people and they have all one language, and this is only the beginning of what they will do, and now nothing they have imagined they can do will be impossible for them." In the beginning, it appeared the product's unity was for the greater good; however, the motive behind their quest for unity was to seek glory for themselves. And so, from this, we learn that the power of unity can be used for good as well as for evil and that not all unity is for the good of mankind, regardless of how it appears.

The greatest example of unity to emulate is the Holy Trinity. The Father, the Son, and the Holy Spirit work together as one. This is unity in its purest form. In Genesis 1:26, the Manufacturer (God) says, "...Let us make man...." Each Person of the Trinity had a vital role to play in the creation of and redemption plan for the Product. Each Person knew His responsibility. Each Person had a role to fulfill. Each Person contributed, because each Person understood the power of unity. This level of unity is a depiction of the principles and characteristics of the Manufacturer. Since the product is made in the image and after the likeness of the Godhead, unity is a reflection of the Creator. This is the unity the product must emulate.

Unfortunately, the spirit released into the earth when Adam sinned changed the dynamics of unity. The emphasis of the product was no longer connected to the principles of the Manufacturer. The product's (man) objective shifted to making a name for himself. This was depicted in Genesis 11: 4-6, with the construction of the Tower of Babel.

Where there is no unity, disunity emerges, and as a result it produces division. When division takes root, the priority becomes every man for himself, or self-preservation. There is no resolution, because everyone has his own agenda.

Throughout history, wars have been won by individuals coming together on one accord, with the same agenda, focused, determined and committed in a unified front to accomplish a set goal, reach an objective, and win the war. If a corporation, a family, or a nation is to be successful, where everyone benefits, there has to be unity. There has to be a change of heart, where the focus is not "I," but "we," not "what can you do for me?" but "what can I do for the good of the whole?"

The Manufacturer showed us the importance of unity. He showed us the way. When we are walking together in the purest form, we are depicting the Holy Trinity. When we do not, we allow division to take root. Walking together, we stand. Not walking together, we fail.

As you read this book, and recall history as you know it, ask yourself this question: When have we walked together?

Chapter One

Religion ~ The Product's Solution to Reconnect to the Manufacturer

Many have often wondered why the Manufacturer (God) in Genesis 11 scattered the product when the product attempted to build a tower that would reach the heavens. After all, it states that the whole earth had one language and one speech (Genesis 11:1). In the Manufacturer's eyes, this was open rebellion against Him. The Manufacturer knew that the product's desire for unity had the potential for great evil, because the underlying motive for building the tower was not unity, but pride.

Since the Tower of Babel, the product has continued to seek a name for himself. Thousands of years later, we see that the product's quest for unity is now portrayed in another facade—religion. One of the major reasons for this was the product's shift to the establishment of stratified societies, or caste systems. These systems were rooted and grounded in bigotry, prejudice, and exclusion.

A caste system is a social structure in which classes are determined by heredity, social status, or wealth. A pure caste system is a closed system, which allows little or no change. It is generally described as any groups of people that combine some or all elements of endogamy (marriage within the family), hereditary transmission of occupation, and status in a hierarchy.[1] Stratified societies were historically organized in Europe in which distinctive privileges sanctioned by law or social mores were confined to only that specific social subset of the society, and were inherited automatically by the offspring.[2]

---

1 1-2, 4-6. Social Caste. < http://encl.tfode.com/social-caste#Europe>
2 8,115. Social Caste. < http://encl.tfode.com/social-caste#Europe>

The makers of The European caste system, or feudalism, were cunning and divisive, making assessments which over-valued some, while devaluing others. By doing this, they failed to consider what Genesis 1:26 says, "And God said, let us [Father, Son, and Holy Spirit] make mankind in our image, after our likeness, and let them have complete authority over the fish of the sea, the birds of the air, the [tame] beasts, and over all the earth, and over everything that creeps upon the earth."

Absent from the original assignment given in Genesis 1:26 is having complete authority over another person or ethnic group. Unfortunately, the involvement of the Church in the implementation of the caste system made it appear the Manufacturer changed His mind. The presence of many church leaders' involvement gave validity to the system, implying the Manufacturer sanctioned it. The significance of this affected Europe, which impacted the standard for colonization, and established the new paradigm-religion. Religion was vital in the establishment of European civilization, culture and society as a whole. And because of its influence, the Europeans who colonized other countries, including the new nation, took the same position, a position rooted and grounded in the bowels of religion.

Religion is defined as a belief in the existence of a divine power or powers to be obeyed and worshiped as the creator and ruler of the universe.[3] The problem with this definition is that it limits the Divine Power. It does not express whether or not the Divine Power cares or loves His creations. It does not address the value of relationship and His unconditional love. It fails to mention that He is Omnipotent, Omniscient, and that He is Self-Sufficient. Religion is the attempt to reconnect the Product to the Manufacturer. The problem with this is that the product is not equipped to recognize its failures and flaws. The Manufacturer made the product; therefore, only the Manufacturer knows when the product is sick and not

---

3   The American Heritage College Dictionary, Third Ed. (Boston-New York: Houghlin Mifflin Company, 1993) p.1153

functioning according to the original plan. Only the Manufacturer's original plan can reconnect the product back to Him.

The hand of religion forced itself throughout Europe, and the world. It was like an invading army, conquering, and consuming everything it touched. It had the appearance of truth, so the assumption was that it was truth. It sought to be all things for all nations, but it rejected the only means of salvation when it excluded Jesus Christ as being divine and the only Son of the Manufacturer. Thus, the revelation was hidden and each ethnic group was allowed to create its own truth. The amazing thing is that none of these so called truths addressed the spiritual condition of the product, which was originally caused by the broken relationship with the Manufacturer.

As a result of this broken relationship, the product became contaminated. Again, religion was the attempt to fix this. But religion cannot address the spiritual needs of the product. It cannot heal the product. The product is a spirit that resides in a body and has a soul. The spiritual needs must be met first if the product is to be restored; otherwise, the contaminated spirit will always be a source of contention. This is where religion has failed.

Religion is one of the sources that feed the product's heart, because it seeks to bypass the spirit man. Religion fails to understand that the product is attracted to either the spirit of light or the spirit of darkness. John 4:24 states, "God is a Spirit (a spiritual Being) and those who worship Him must worship Him in spirit and in truth (reality)." They that worship the enemy worship him in lies, and in darkness. The Manufacturer is the rock. His work is perfect. All of His ways and His laws are just. He is a God of faithfulness without breach, or deviation, and He never misses the mark. Jesus expressed the heart of the enemy in John 8:44, "You are of your father, the devil, and it is your will to practice the lusts and gratify the desires [which are characteristics] of your father. He was a murderer from the beginning and does not stand in truth, because there is no truth in him. When he speaks a falsehood, he speaks what is natural to him, for he is a liar [himself] and the father of lies and of all that is false." This is a powerful indictment. The enemy chose to reject Truth and authority. He chose to establish falsehood. Religion is his greatest sales pitch because religion acknowledges the Manufacturer, but rejects His principles.

The strength of religion has ingeniously molded itself into each culture so that each ethnic group sees religion as the protector of their identity. In other words, religion protects their name and perpetuates their specific society. In every society or in every ethnic group, religion takes on a different persona by borrowing from each culture. Its longevity is predicated upon bringing gratification to each group that buys into its doctrine.

Adam missed the mark when he rejected Truth and embraced lies. His sin placed him in opposition to the Source of light, and darkness was the place where he landed. In Romans 6:23, it says, "For the wages of sin is death, but the gift of God is eternal life through Jesus Christ our Lord." The wages consist of the inferior reality of this world, while rejecting the superior reality of Truth. This action forced the product into an "existing" mode rather than a "living" mode. Life provided by Jesus Christ produces productivity; whereas, sin produces just existing. Therefore, since the product was created to live and be productive, the product maximizes the productivity of death produced by sin. Genesis 2:17 states, "But of the tree of the knowledge of good and evil, thou shalt not eat of it: for in the day that thou eatest thereof thou shalt surely die." The product began to die as a result of eating of the tree. The abundant life was removed, and was off limits until the coming of the Lord Jesus Christ.

Sin uses religion as a means of establishing wedges and bitterness, yet it remains anonymous in the process. This occurs because of the bond between religion and sin; religion produces blindness, and sin exercises authority. Paul makes a powerful statement regarding blindness in Ephesians 4:18-19, he says, "Their moral understanding is darkened and their reasoning is beclouded. [They are] alienated [estranged, self banished] from life of God [with no share in it; this is] because of the ignorance (the want of knowledge and perception, the willful blindness) that is deep-seated in them, due to their hardness of heart [to the insensitiveness of their moral nature]. In their spiritual apathy they have become callous and past feeling and reckless and have abandoned themselves [a prey] to unbridled sensuality, eager and greedy to indulge in every form of impurity [that their depraved desires may suggest and demand]."

Sin has seized every opportunity presented to it. It is a master of exploitation. Sin does not just want to participate; it wants to rule with impunity. Ruling with impunity requires it to overwhelm the product with lies so that the product buys into its reality. This is achieved through subtle means whereby the Truth is defined as a lie, and a lie is conveyed as Truth. This is evident in Genesis 3:4-5, "But the serpent said to the woman, you shall not surely die. For God knows that in the day you eat of it your eyes will be opened and you will be like God, knowing the difference between good and evil and blessing and calamity."

Eve failed to remember that they were created in the image and likeness of the Manufacturer; therefore, they had all that they needed. The Manufacturer never left the product; however, the product's sin placed a demand on the Manufacturer to remove the product from the garden, "So God drove out the product, and placed at the east of the garden of Eden the cherubim and a flaming sword which turned every way to keep and guard the way to the tree of life," (Genesis 3:24). This was done to prevent the product from eating of the tree of life, which would have placed the product in an eternal state, or position whereby the product could not be redeemed. The coming of Jesus Christ was to reestablish relationship and not to create religion. Only the law of the spirit of life in Christ Jesus can restore the product back to the original position.

Every spirit sent to the earth in a body has potential, purpose and a destiny. However, through the support of the caste system, the product sought and executed plans to undermine this principle, which is a violation of the Word, and violation of the Word means the product has parity or has risen to the level of equality with the Manufacturer. This attitude of wanting equality with the Manufacturer reflects the heart of Lucifer, the origin of the power of darkness. His attitude was driven by pride. His pride places great emphasis on himself as recorded in Isaiah 14: 13-14, "And you said in your heart, I will ascend to heaven; I will exalt my throne above the stars of God; I will sit upon the mount of assembly in the uttermost north. I will ascend above the heights of the clouds; I will make myself like the Most High."

With this mindset, the product has placed the Manufacturer in a box, whereby the product defines Him by the means of religion. Thus, the product pushes religion instead of truth. The Thirty Year's War is a classic example of the product seeking his own way, and rejecting Truth. The efforts to spread religious ideals grew more militant, while spreading Truth was lost in the equation. Religion became the rule, while Truth was the exception. This pattern remains intact today. Solutions are not established through dialog, but by confrontation. History has shown that all the Wars of Religion were the result of confrontation, because religion, in a subtle way embraces the same concept as democracy, which is the majority rule. In other words, religion, as well as democracy, seeks to establish changes by revolution instead of resolution.

Revolution divides; resolution unifies. Revolution comes from the bottom up; resolution is from the top down. Revolution is of the product; resolution is of the Manufacturer. Religion has never been equipped to address the challenges that face the product, because it is based on the product's effort to reconnect to the Manufacturer. If every recommendation by religion was implemented, there would be a deficiency in the product because one-third of the makeup of the product is spirit. Again, religion is incapable of eradicating the sickness of the spirit. The sickness of the product lies deeply in the spirit of the product. Religion focuses on the fruit; however, true healing requires destroying the root. This can only be achieved by the One who made the product, and knows how it was designed to function.

The caste system in Europe extended its hand to the new land in the guise of freedom, but concealed in religion. Externally, the package looked extremely appealing; but internally, it was filled with confusion, deception, disdain, demoralization, abortion, and insensitivity. These traits drive religion and become the seeds that breed division. Consequently, religion has a built in system that is programmed to be in opposition to Truth. Remember, though religion is the product's attempt at restoration, it is, in fact, the enemy to relationship. The belief in religion removes the possibility of relationship. Religion is so structural that it believes in the existence of a supreme being that rules, but it does not give the product the opportunity to have a relationship with Him. Much of the emphasis is placed on the product "doing" instead of "being." Performing good deeds neither restores connection, nor enables the product to identify with the Manufacturer.

From early history to the present, religion has played a major role in bringing about division and instability. It actually began the day Adam fell in the garden, and this fall has impacted humanity. The objective of religion was to restore connection while circumventing the principles of the Manufacturer. Thus, religion sought to establish its own rules for healing and restoration. To add to the deception, each religion has its own view about the traits of the Supreme Being. In the eyes of some, the Supreme Being's power exceeds his love. In the eyes of others, His love exceeds His power. There is no clear definition of His character; therefore, there is no definitive process or directive for restoration. Some religions see the Supreme Being as "she," others as "he." This confusion wreaks havoc and prevents unity. Unity is a product of clarity, but confusion produces division. Division is inherent to religion, in that religion seeks to elevate itself by equating itself with Christianity.

The stronghold of religion has remained throughout human history, and has become progressively rooted in the product's mind. Freedom of religion was the motivating factor as to why the founders of this nation sought a new land; thus, religion became the model, and not the Words of the Manufacturer. Religion releases a mob mentality when it is faced with opposition. Again, this has been its pattern throughout history. The Crusades and the Thirty Year's War are examples of this. In each attempt to spread religious ideologies, the outcome was defeat and failure, because intimidation, rather than love, was the weapon of warfare,[4] and the manifestation of the "authority of the people" was the focal point. Thus, religion became a liability, not an asset, and not the solution to reconnect to the Manufacturer.

---

4   Ferguson and Bruun, p. 203-212 and p. 425-433; Chambers et al, p.357-368 and p. 523-527

Chapter Two
Religion and the Authority of the People

Religion played a significant role in establishing the new nation. The value the founders placed on religion has pulled the country in many directions. The founders felt compelled to place more emphasis on the "authority of the people" than the authority of the Manufacturer. In the book, *The American Promise, a History of the United States, Volume 1*, it states that in May 1776, the Congress in Philadelphia recommended that all states draw up a constitution based on the "the authority of the people."[5] Consciously, the founders were saying the will of the people takes priority over the will of the Manufacturer. This is part of the paradigm of Europe. Europeans used the church as the model; whereas, the new nation used the people as the model. However, in each case, the Manufacturer's value is modified and decreased. By doing this, it appears that the product desires to share in His glory. This attitude was expressed in the thoughts of the founders of this nation, except the shift was from "I" to "We the People."

Anything or person that seeks to share His glory is in violation of the Word (Isaiah 42:8). The Manufacturer is self-sufficient, and He is God all by Himself. His credibility rests in His word, for He has magnified His word above His name. With the "authority of the people" as the foundation structure, the elevation of the product put the product in a position to become idolized. Thus, worshipping the church and the people became self-perpetuating standards. The citizens of the new world were greatly influenced by the leaders in Europe, but the founders sought to add a measure of protection that placed them above the pattern in Europe by stating,

---

5   Roark et al, p.171

"That all men are by nature equally free and independent..."[6]

The product then went on to assert "In God We Trust" on the currency and as the nation's motto to acknowledge his commitment to the Manufacturer. Acknowledging and putting trust in the Manufacturer is commendable, but His principles must have preeminence over religion and the doctrine of the product. As long as the doctrine of the product takes precedence over the principles of the Manufacturer, the Manufacturer is not the one being trusted. This was evident in the early stages of this nation, and it has continued until today. While the product advocated the importance of trusting in God, their trust and adherence to the principles of the Manufacturer were not reflected in their treatment of others.

For example, one of the criterions for establishing the rights of the people was owning land. This was one of the qualifications for determining one's value and ability to lead. This requirement eliminated one-quarter to one-half of all adult white males, besides African Americans, Native Americans, and women. One of the founding fathers, John Adams, urged the framers of Massachusetts to disregard the scope of suffrage, and to adopt a traditional view that excluded non-whites and women.[7] It must be assumed that John Adams forgot to read Acts 17:26 where it states, "And he made from one [common origin, one source, one blood] all nations of men to settle on the face of the earth..." He not only made the product from the same blood, but all the nations (ethnic groups) on the face of the earth are redeemed by the same blood. Since the blood that created all was not inferior, neither was the blood that redeemed all inferior; therefore, one ethnic group cannot be inferior to another. Unfortunately, accepting the inferiority theory has been a hindrance in the area of race, class, and gender relationships. Again, its origin is from the power of darkness, which has been influencing humanity since the fall of Adam.

---

6 Virginia Bill of Rights, cited in Roark et al, p. 171
7 Roark et al, p. 172

The founders of this nation failed to recognize that their attitude was an expression of a spirit, and this spirit was not the spirit of the Manufacturer. This spirit was rooted and grounded in pride, selfishness and intolerance. A reflection of this intolerance is expressed by George Mason, author of *The Virginia Bill of Rights*. He owned over one hundred slaves, but none benefited from his statement that "all men are by nature equally free and independent."[8] The Founders of this nation placed a high value on morality, but failed to practice what they preached. As a result, the prince of the power of darkness took advantage of every step made by the founders to set up his kingdom; the creation of The Declaration of Independence, Bill of Rights, and the United States Constitution, provided him the needed access. The product's desires expressed in these documents were honorable, but honor without substance will never achieve the objective, and that substance can only come from the Manufacturer.

The Declaration of Independence was a commendable, courageous act, but independence should never be the objective of the product. Since the proclamation "In God We Trust" is on the currency, the conclusion is that, as a nation and as individuals, we must constantly depend on the Source that created us. Our sight should be on things above. Colossians 3:1-3 states, "If then you have been raised with Christ [to a new life, thus sharing His resurrection from the dead], aim at and seek the [rich, eternal treasures] that are above, where Christ is, seated at the right hand of God. And set your minds and keep them set on what is above (the higher things), not on the things that are on the earth. For [as far as this world is concerned] you have died, and your [new real] life is hidden with Christ in God." The truest form of independence is to depend on the One that created you in His image and after His likeness.

---

8   Roark et al, p.172

The essence of the Constitution of the United States is expressed in the Preamble: "We the People, in order to form a more perfect union, establish justice, insure domestic tranquility, provide for the common defense, promote the general welfare, and secure the blessings of liberty to ourselves and our posterity, do ordain and establish this Constitution for these United States of America." [9] These are powerful words that require powerful leadership. The leadership must take on a higher dimension, transcending humanity, going beyond every aspiration of the written word. Justice must be established through the eyes of the Manufacturer. Therefore, the product must make a conscious effort to rise above every circumstance and situation. Fulfilling this awesome assignment required the founders to look to a Source greater than themselves. If this had been the objective from the outset, many things could have been accomplished. Unless there is a commitment to enforce the laws, the laws in themselves are like clouds without rain.

Unless the Product submits totally to the Creator, all of his efforts will be in vain. Proverbs 14:34 states, "Uprightness and right standing with God (moral and spiritual rectitude in every area and relation) elevate a nation, but sin is a reproach to any people." The Constitution of these United States cannot take the place of the written Word. Since the Constitution was promulgated by the product, it can be circumvented by the product. The Constitution is not above reproach; it has to be implemented by humans that are flawed. The words of The Creator are above reproach; they do not change, and neither can they be circumvented. The bottom line is this: the Bill of Rights, Declaration of Independence and the Constitution of these United States are at the mercy of those that enforce them. If the hearts of those enforcing the law are corrupt, the law will not be executed fairly and equally. The nation can declare itself "the land of the free, and home of the brave," ("Star-Spangled Banner") or that we are "one nation under God;" (the Pledge of Allegiance) however, words require commitment, discipline and dedication.

---

9 Roark et al, p. A-3

The founders were vague and indecisive in their commitment to the words depicted in the Constitution, where it states, "All men are created equal." However, the subject of equality was never an issue with the Manufacturer. Humanity was created in His image and likeness. Humanity must discover and accept this truth. Truth cannot be discovered in religion. Truth must be revealed by the Source of truth. It must be expressed in all aspects of life. The founders had a zeal for the Manufacturer, but the zeal was not according to knowledge. Knowledge would have revealed that Jesus is the way, the truth, and the life. Knowledge would have revealed that the "authority of people" presents an erroneous view. Humanity was created in the image of the Godhead; therefore, all ethnic groups were created from the same design. The Manufacturer expressed His desire in what He created, so no ethnic group was created inferior or superior to another. By asserting that all men were created equal, the founders left the impression that the Manufacturer was not clear in His annunciation, thus they sought to bring clarity to the matter.

Historic documents and the laws of this nation have not addressed the deficit of Truth and Light. Again, each sought to address the needs of the physical product and the soul, leaving the spirit out of the loop. The truth is that each ethnicity is created from the same Source. However, it appears at many junctures in the country's history, this truth was compromised. Further, the country established its case by proclaiming to be a nation that trusts in God. If it is, then it has to be a nation that reflects the principles and characteristics of Jesus.

1 John 2:9 established the criterion for the Christian walk, "Whoever says he is in the light and [yet] hates his brother [Christian, born-again child of God his Father] is in darkness even until now." Then, in 1 John 1: 6-7 it says, "[So] if we say we are partakers together and enjoy fellowship with Him when we live and move and are walking about in darkness, we are [both] speaking falsely and do not live and practice the truth [which the gospel

presents]. But if we [really] are living and walking in Light as He [Himself] is in Light, we have [true, unbroken] fellowship with one another, and the blood of Jesus Christ His Son cleanses (removes) us from all sin and guilt [keeps us cleansed from sin in all its forms and manifestations]." Walking in these principles is the measuring stick of our true conviction. Words are easy to say, but action requires commitment, and the commitment must consider the spirit man.

The Bill of Rights, which consists of the first ten amendments of the Constitution, guarantees certain rights, among which are the freedoms of assembly and religion.[10] These rights addressed only the physical and soul man; the spirit was completely removed from the equation. The principles of the Manufacturer regarding these freedoms were not taken into consideration. The Declaration of Independence was designed to free the colonies from Great Britain, but the nation maintained the spirit of the caste system. The Constitution was a mandated guideline, but was executed by flawed individuals whose hearts were corrupt, filled with all forms of bitterness, hatred, and prejudice. This revelation was evident with the founders as well as those that administered the law. What the leaders failed to consider is that the principles of the Manufacturer are superior to the laws of the product. The product cannot function according to its purpose without complying with the principles outlined in the manual created by the Manufacturer.

The First Amendment in the Constitution provides for freedom of religion and their rights to assemble and to petition the Government. The First Amendment guarantee of freedom of religion has two clauses: the "free exercise clause," which allows individuals to practice or not practice any religion, and the "establishment clause," which prevents the federal government from discriminating against or favoring any particular religion.[11] This amendment creates division by giving rights to all religions. This amend-

---

10   Divine et al, p. 177-178
11   Roark et al, p. A-9

ment demonstrates the founding fathers were guided by the concept of "the authority of the people." People are individuals who have a variety of beliefs. Under the First Amendment, Christianity is thrown into the same barrel as religion; therefore, each belief system has the same equal rights.[12]

One of the strongest traits of Christianity is the presence of power in demonstration (1st Corinthians 2:4) - the power to love, and the power to recognize truth and embrace it. The Power to exercise authority in the earth is based on the complete work of Jesus Christ. This authority exceeds the "authority of the people." This explains why the "authority of people" wreaks havoc, while the authority based on the words of the Manufacturer releases love, relationship, unity, and peace that surpasses all understanding (Philippians 4:7). The concept of the "authority of the people" says, in essence, that the product can fix itself, and therein lies the problem. The product has never been in a position to fix itself. The product was created by the Manufacturer. In other words, the Superior created the inferior. True authority and power must be released by the Manufacturer. Again, a unified product is still inferior to the Manufacturer.

Jesus provided the way. He is the truth, and He is the light (John 14:6). Christianity is all about Him. The power, as well as the authority is released through Him. This authority is from the Father, who is the Self-Sufficient One, and the All-Knowing One. The "authority of the people" is motivated by a selfish attitude and a lack of Truth and understanding. It is also motivated by culture, ethnicity, and a disobedient spirit that was released when Adam failed. Remember, the product is contaminated with his religious belief, and his religious belief seeks to reduce the creditability of Christianity. This explains why Christianity has been placed in the same barrel as religion. The enemy to truth was very clever in arranging this setup. Again, the wars in the early 17th century were not about Christianity.

---

12 Roark et al, p. A-9

They were, instead, appropriately titled: "Religious Wars."[13]

The finished work of the Lord Jesus Christ has provided freedom. Freedom is so entrenched in Him that He gave His life. He became the Emancipator for all humanity. Maintaining a system that is in violation of His principles exposes the hearts of those engaged in it. Their hearts are saying that their personal ideology, supported by religion has priority over His words and His truth. This eases the conscience of the product to separate from the Manufacturer's and establish his own truth; but, regardless of the reasoning, "the authority of the people" can never take the place of the Manufacturer.

---

13 Ferguson and Bruun, p. 464

Chapter Three
A Nation Divided

The history of the United States reveals that years after the Constitution was ratified, the nation was divided in many areas. Both the separation from Great Britain and the implementation of the "authority of the people" failed to cease the division. There was a division between the north, the south, and the new territories on the issue of slavery.[14] The birth of the Industrial Revolution also contributed to the division, because the gap between the rich and poor grew wider, emulating Europe under the caste system.[15] In addition, the gap between the educated and the uneducated brought on another facet of division. Because there was an absence of Godly leadership, and the Manufacturer was not allowed to reign freely, division continued to run rampant.

Division is a reflection of the rebellious spirit controlled by the power of darkness. This rebellious spirit seeks to focus on self, and on everything that brings self-pleasure and self-fulfillment. It repels truth, righteousness, and holiness. This mentality reveals the state of helplessness the product is in when Truth is rejected. Truth produces unity for those that seek it; whereas, division is the result when Truth is rejected. Rejecting truth not only produces an inferior plan and purpose for the product, but the product's view becomes distorted, and his eyes are blinded. Ephesians 4:18 gives a clear understanding of the depth of blindness, "Their moral understanding is darkened and their reasoning is beclouded. [They are] alienated (estranged, self-banished) from the life of God [with no share in it; this is] because of the ignorance (the want of knowledge and perception, the willful blindness) that is deep-seated in them, due to their hardness of heart [to

---

14   Divine et al, p. 382-409
15   Spielvogel, p. 716-717, 721-722

the insensitiveness of their moral nature]."

This mentality is connected to pride, jealousy, prejudice, racism, suspicion, envy, and insensitivity. These are the traits of the power of darkness, preventing the product from recognizing Truth. Truth penetrates the veils of selfishness and self-righteousness. Without Truth, the product can justify pride, which produces jealousy and always elevates itself above others. Jealously produces prejudice, justifying racist views of superiority, which prompts the elevation of one's self, or ethnicity. This elevation produces a suspicious spirit towards others. These traits have influenced humanity since the fall of Adam.

The Manufacturer sent the first man, Adam. His assignment was to be fruitful and multiply, replenish the earth, subdue and have dominion (Genesis 1:28). Adam failed his assignment, because he failed to exercise that dominion over the serpent (Genesis 3). As a result of his failure, the product became disconnected from the Manufacturer. The Manufacturer sent the last Adam, Jesus Christ, who completed His assignment, and the product has the opportunity to be reconnected to the Manufacturer. The reconnection is predicated on accepting the finished work of the Son. The product could not reconnect through its own means, so the Manufacturer had to establish the perimeters by which the product could be reconnected. Any other effort by the product was fruitless, because he was contaminated, and this status could not be changed by the product. Therefore, the product's only means of addressing the challenges and changes was through revolution. Again, revolution does not necessarily produce resolution. The Civil War is a classic example. It was a war pitting natural brother against natural brother, and spiritual brother against spiritual brother. Many lives were lost, but a resolution was not achieved.

Many historians have stated that slavery was not the sole motive behind this war. It was a combination of politics, economics, and religion. From a political and economic standpoint, President Lincoln's objective was to keep the union together.[16] The Abolitionists were strong in their denouncement of slavery, and this was the catalyst that brought slavery to the forefront.[17] However, it was not out of some deep remorse or fear of pending doom. Instead, this was a process where Godly men and women chose to stand in the gap for a nation.[18] However, contrary to popular opinion, the removal of slavery was not the desire of the masses.[19]

Religion was a major factor leading up to the war. Its chief purpose was to maintain the status quo; whereas, Truth would have exposed the status quo. Religion packaged and sold the idea that the Manufacturer was an abusive father by embracing the notion that one ethnic group was superior to another; but, one of the greatest examples of abuse is a father favoring one child over another. The product, because of the divided state the nation was in, believed that this was the correct road to take. The result was a nation divided, thus civil war.

The Civil War was one of the most horrific acts in human history, slaughtering many and aborting the potential of even more. However, the seeds that produced this crop were planted long before this harvest. The power of sin that produced the death of Abel (Genesis 4:8) stretched forth its hand and touched a young nation, bringing brother against brother. Slavery, religion, culture, education, and economics were all contributing factors that added to the conflict. These divisions were initiated for the sole purpose of exploiting all sides. The convictions of each group was so deeply rooted and grounded that neither side saw the light. Neither side was willing to trust the Source that they confessed and abide by the Truth that was already established. The Source that they confessed had already stated His position regarding the matter, and that was that out of one blood He made all nations and ethnic groups.

---

16 Roark et al, p. 364
17 Franklin and Moss, p. 188
18 Divine et al, p. 315-317
19 Roark et al, p 323-349

The opposing positions taken leading up to the war did not express the desire of the Manufacturer. The product made a decision to take matters into his own hands, disregarding the principles of the Manufacturer, resulting in no firm or fixed resolution because the product was seeking resolutions based on what is seen. The picture that is seen in the natural does not reveal the real story. There is a spirit behind that which is seen; however, the effort of the product focused on what was seen [the fruit] while the root remained the same. Removing the fruit gives the product some means of satisfaction, but because the roots remain, satisfaction quickly turns into frustration. Frustration, the result from the rejection of Authority, breeds contempt, and contempt forces the product farther away from the Manufacturer. This nation fit the paradigm for this great deception. As a matter of fact, the founders cooperated completely by buying into the notion that Christianity and religion were one in the same.

The Civil War was the result of religious ideals, and not spiritual truth. It was a war in which the ideology of the product took precedence over the principles of the Manufacturer. It was motivated by erroneous thinking supported by religious ideals that had its origin in the early century. It was birthed out of deception, personal opinions, and desires to elevate one ethnic group over another. It said, in essence, that one group believed it had a corner on truth, defying the principles of the Manufacturer. This is evident in some of the traditions and laws established by the product, such as the Black Codes, which were created during the period after the Civil War called Reconstruction.[20] They did not reflect the principles of the Manufacturer, but the will of the people. Such laws and traditions promulgated and motivated by the desires of a specific group of people reflected the natural instead of the spiritual realm.

The words of The Declaration of Independence states, "We hold these truths to be self-evident, that all men are created equal, that they are endowed by

---

20 Franklin and Moss, p. 206

their Creator with certain unalienable Rights, that among these are Life, Liberty, and the Pursuit of Happiness."[21] One must ask, when the founders of this nation were scripting the words of this document, did the contents of these words apply to all, regardless of race, creed, religion, ethnicity, or gender, or only to a select few? This question has never been answered.

Because of the words in this profound document, the world looked upon this nation as the model for social justice and equality, and as the place where individual potential can be released with minimal opposition. Based on these words, this should be a nation where citizens of every ethnic group, regardless of their background or social status should expect to be treated with dignity and respect. The only problem with this was that it was based on a fallacy. The words of this profound document were written by men whose hearts were corrupted. So, although they were beautiful words, they were words without substance.

The environment and attitude prior to the Civil War revealed the product's ineptitude in complying with his own laws. The scripture is very clear on this matter, as stated in Proverbs 14:12, "There is a way which seems right to a man and appears straight before him, but at the end of it is the way of death." Spiritual death occurred before the physical death. The nation was spiritually dead as it related to the subject of slavery. The heart of each side of the Civil War was without power, because each was controlled by the "authority of the people." Again, spiritual death preceded physical death.

An absence of Light contributed to the chaos that existed, pitting brother against brother, following the pattern of Cain (Genesis 4: 5-10). Providing light is the responsibility of the church (Matthew 5:14). Sadly, a significant portion of the Church was so deeply rooted in tradition that she surrendered her ability to produce light. Remember, Light brings illumination, and it exposes the heart and attitude of the Manufacturer (John 2:46 &

---

21 Roark et al, p. A-1

49). An absence of light places the product in a position whereby darkness rules with impunity.

To reiterate, darkness is the source of division, bigotry, and prejudice. The spirit of darkness that reigned over the nation during this period refused to reach a Godly conclusion before the war. It was so deeply rooted in the hearts of individuals that thousands on both sides aborted their potential, forfeited their purpose, and missed their destiny. This includes those who acted with abolitionist John Brown on the night of October 16, 1859, when they invaded Harpers Ferry, Virginia in a failed attempt to end slavery via revolution. This band of individuals gave their lives for what they believed was a worthy cause. Slavery could not be abolished by revolution; it had to start in the heart of all. John Brown's courageous stand on that infamous night is to be commended, but Mr. Brown's position did not reflect the heart of the Manufacturer, or the heart of Jesus. This action focused on the fruit and not the root; consequently, the residue of the root remains with us today.

In retrospect, the Civil War was not a war between the states based on slavery, but on the fact the nation failed to execute its own laws and rules. This war was an expression of the bitter heart of a nation. Those seeking to glorify the resolve, strength, character, and heart of the nation, failed to understand the corruption of the heart, the influence of darkness, and their own self-serving attitude. Thus, romantic depictions of the nation are portrayed instead of the truth. The best way to define true romance is a love affair between two individuals who share mutual respect and the same value system of justice, morals and decency. Using this as the foundation, true romance would be predicated not just on the intent, but also on the action; not on the letter of the law, but on execution of the law. The best example of true love is the Manufacturer sending His only Son to redeem the product He created in His own image (1 John 4: 10-11).

The Bible is clear on the importance of counting the cost before starting something (Luke 14:28). What is the cost for courage, truth and commitment? Just as there is price for obtaining freedom, there is a greater price for the daily commitment to preserve that which has been obtained. Too often more emphasis is placed on the lives lost in protecting the Constitution than on the lives lost seeking to fulfill the essence of the Constitution. John Brown and his followers clearly saw themselves as protectors, whose job was to ensure the fulfillment of the Constitution. The American Revolution, as well as all wars fought before the Civil War, was necessary to protect freedom from outside sources. John Brown and his disciples fought to protect the Constitution from inside forces. However, each failed to grasp that the greatest enemy was the condition of the heart.

Religion had its strongholds throughout the nation. Prior to the war, neither side was willing to allow the Words of the Manufacturer to have the final say. Religion failed in maintaining unity. It was, however, instrumental in dividing the nation to such a degree that war was inevitable. Missed was the golden opportunity to allow the Manufacturer to resolve the conflict. Since there is but One Father, and everybody is a brother, as it related to the war, why would brothers fight against one another since there is but one family? Why would the lives of over six-hundred thousand be destroyed from the same family?[22] If religion was successful, the war between brothers would not have taken place. In fact, if religion was successful, and all are brothers, why would one brother take advantage of another? Why would one brother think that he is better than another brother based on skin color?

In the Gettysburg Address, President Abraham Lincoln stated, "government of the people, by the people, and for the people shall not perish from the earth."[23] This statement was spoken without the understanding that the product, within himself, could not save himself. However, because the

---

22 Boyer et al, p. 477
23 Divine et al, p. 415

statement was made by a credible person, the consensus of the nation is that this statement is a statement of truth. Thus, the product has fallen for the bait and ends up committing to something that is impossible for him to accomplish.

The product should heed what Paul wrote to the Philippians church in Philippians 4:13: "I have strength for all things in Christ who empowers me [I am ready for anything and equal to anything through Him who infuses inner strength into me; I am self-sufficient in Christ's sufficiency." The founders, as well as President Lincoln, must have either forgotten or rejected this statement. The sufficiency is not in the "authority of the people," but in the Lord Jesus Christ. The founders acknowledged and proclaimed their allegiance to the Manufacturer, but their actions revealed what was in their hearts. Jesus expressed it this way in Luke 6:45: "A good man out of the good treasure of his heart bringeth forth that which is good; and an evil man out of the evil treasure of his heart bringeth forth that which is evil: for of the abundance of the heart his mouth speaketh."

The good heart that produces good fruit impacts the total product. The word "good" denotes "beneficial,"[24] as in beneficial to all citizens. Laws must be enforced to ensure that justice avails itself to all. The laws and rules were created for citizens; the citizens were not created for the rules and laws. The Constitution and the Declaration of Independence were created with potential; but, in many cases, this potential was aborted, because the product refused to check his heart and give it to the Manufacturer.

While much emphasis was placed on slavery as being the catalyst for the Civil War, disunity, disagreement, envy and the caste system were already in the minds of the leadership. The opinions and concepts of the product were fueled by their religious belief, which had overwhelmed the heart (the guiding system of the Product). Therefore, war was inevitable, not because

---

24 The American Heritage College Dictionary, p. 586

of slavery, but due to the condition of the product's heart. The product had a heart condition that only the Manufacturer could heal, because the product's heart was divided.

Chapter Four

The Heart of the Founding Fathers

King David was wise enough to recognize the condition of his heart. He gave the Manufacturer permission to search him thoroughly for all faults, errors, blemishes, calamities and impurities (Psalm 139: 23-24). Only the Creator of a person or thing knows why it is created, and how it is supposed to function. Proverbs 4:23 says, "Keep and guard your heart with all vigilance and above all that you guard, for out of it flow the springs of life." The heart must first be given to the Manufacturer. Once He has searched and changed the heart, the product must maintain what He has provided. A heart that is not guarded becomes an open door to the enemy. As we can plainly see, the enemy has been causing destruction since the fall of Adam. Adam gave the enemy access, and the heart continues to reject and gravitate towards lies and darkness.

The corrupt heart has shaped the foundation of this nation from its inception. It continues to reap a harvest from the seed of deception planted years ago. The major aspect of this harvest was aborting potential. Every spirit sent to earth in a body has potential. Abortion removes the potential and silences the voice of purpose. The church rises up in righteous indignation over physical abortion, but is less active after the product is born. Aborting the product before birth is a great evil; however, the evil of aborting the product's potential after birth is just as great. Abortion in any form is ungodly and evil. The caste system, slavery, ethnic cleansing, discrimination, and bigotry are tools used to abort potential after the product is born.

Unity in its purest form begins in the heart. In Jeremiah 17: 9-10, it says, "The heart is deceitful above all things, and it is exceedingly perverse and corrupt and severely, mortally sick! Who can know it [perceive, understand, be acquainted with his own heart and mind? I the Lord search the mind, I try the heart, even to give to every man according to his ways, according to the fruit of his doings." Since the fall of Adam, a corrupt heart has been the product's greatest challenge, preventing the product from functioning according to his purpose.

The scripture says the heart of the product is deceitful. It is dishonest, and filled with lies. Under these circumstances, the heart's objective is to deceive. This sickness has become so deeply-rooted, the product is unable to recognize it. While the product sees it as the solution, religion contributes to, as well as helps cover the sickness. Therefore, it is impossible for the product to know the severity of his condition.

Religion is a like applying a bandage on the outside to treat internal bleeding. The result is that it seems like the patient is getting better; but, in reality, the patient is dying. Only the Manufacturer has the skill to search the heart and expose the severity of the matter. This is why religion has played a vital role in the division in the Church, the nation, and the world. The Church seems to be oblivious to the influence of religion, forgetting that her responsibility is to produce light in the world and to be the salt of the earth (Matthew 5:13-14). In many cases, religion is exerting power and authority over the Church, and it should be the other way around.

A corrupt heart says one thing but does the opposite. A corrupt heart is surrounded with darkness and is unable to recognize light. A corrupt heart is so deceived that it values its opinions over the principles of the Manufacturer. This is not a new phenomenon. Adam is the father of this concept. When he was presented with an option, he chose to reject Truth in favor of a lie. Even when Adam was confronted with his act of rebellion, he sought to find an excuse. He blamed his wife (Genesis 3:11-12). This intrinsic nature of the product remains as vindictive today as it was then. The product does not want to own up to his inability to correct himself, but

When Have We Walked TOGETHER?

he continues to blame others to justify his behavior.

The corrupt heart is self-defeating and oblivious to the consequences of its actions. Its actions are based on the spirit that drives it, and it is often ignorant to the devastation of its dilemma. The corruption partners with wickedness and takes on the full nature of darkness. This darkness is rooted and grounded in pride and expresses the characteristics of its father. The prophet Isaiah received divine revelation regarding the consequences of pride: "And you said in your heart, I will ascend to heaven; I will exalt my throne above the stars of God; I will sit upon the mount of assembly in the uttermost north. I will ascend above the heights of the clouds; I will make myself like the most High. Yet you shall be brought down to Sheol (Hades), to the innermost recesses of the pit (the region of the dead)," (Isaiah 14:13-15). The product follows the same pattern as the author of pride, showing this is a heart matter. Once pride takes root in the heart, the heart begins to express its desire and objective. The product then seeks to exalt himself above the Manufacturer.

This explains why this pattern has existed in the product since the fall of Adam. It explains why the laws promulgated by the product failed to reach their goals. It confirms why there is a zeal for the Manufacturer, but the zeal is not according to knowledge (Romans 10:2). It explains why religion has become a substitute for Truth. Religion in a subtle way says, "I will exalt my plans and belief system above the plans and purpose of the Manufacturer." The ways of religion are in opposition to the ways of the Manufacturer. Religion believes that the Manufacturer exists, but that there are many ways to reach him; thus, removing the value of the Lord Jesus Christ. Again, religion is in full compliance with its author to steer its own course.

When everything is about self, there is no room for the feelings, thoughts, and aspiration of others. There has been a change in the heart of the product, so that now, all emphasis is placed on the individual's desires. As a result, the enemy has set up shop in the heart, mind, and the flesh; thus, he has access to the tripartite product. All aspects of the product are available to him and nothing is out of his reach.

The tools that the enemy uses to perform his desires function according to the product's desire and will. Romans 7:15-18 states, "For I do not understand my own actions [I am baffled, bewildered], I do not practice or accomplish what I wish, but I do the very thing that I loathe [which my moral instinct condemns]. Now if I do [habitually] what is contrary to my desires, [that means that] I acknowledge and agree that the law is good (morally excellent) and that I take sides with it. However, it is no longer I who do the deed, but the sin [principle] which is at home in me and has possession of me. For I know that nothing good dwells within me, that is, in my flesh. I can will what is right, but I cannot perform it. [I have the intention and urge to do what is right, but no power to carry it out]." Sin prevents the product from accessing the power that is only controlled by the Manufacturer. This power is released through the Son. The objective of the Son was to re-establish relationship. This could only be achieved when the Son became the product, and paid the ultimate price for sin.

The product now has a choice; but, by making the wrong choice, he remains in the same predicament. Throughout history, the product has been greatly influenced by his culture, ethnicity, and religion. These factors have played a vital role in conditioning the product. The product has a history of making wrong choices, and these wrong choices have expanded the impact of deception. Aligning with Truth produces Godly choices, which requires integrity. There is no greater example of this than the statement in the Declaration of Independence declaring, "We hold these truths to be self-evident, that all men are created equal; that they are endowed by their Creator with certain unalienable rights; that among these are life, liberty, and the pursuit of happiness."[25]

---

25   Roark et al, p. A-1

Again, the question is, does this apply to all or only to a select few? Truth has established that all men are created equally. This equality was not established by the product, but by the Creator. As a result of equality being established, the Creator has placed such value on His product that all are the beneficiaries of gifts, consisting of life, liberty, and the pursuit of happiness. The founders did not provide these gifts. These gifts were a part of the original package. Since the founders did not provide the gifts, the founders are not authorized to rescind the gifts. Access to the gifts enables the product to release potential, fulfill purpose, and reach his or her destiny. It is critical that we understand that no one has the right to rule or dominate another person.

The assignment given to Adam was to exercise dominion over the earth. Genesis 1:28 says, "And God blessed them and said to them, Be fruitful, multiply, and fill the earth, and subdue it [using all its vast resources in the service of God and man]; and have dominion over the fish of the sea, the birds of the air, and over every living creature that moves upon the earth." What is obvious here is the product does not have the authority to rule over another product. Doing so reflects a heart that is out of control and dominated by the power of darkness.

The foundation of the nation was compromised by inferior substances. The inferior substance was religion, and "the authority of the people." The "authority of the people" constructed a Constitution of the United States that failed to bring unity. Let us look at the establishment of a more perfect Union as mentioned in the Preamble to the Constitution. Perfection can not be established by the product. The sins of Adam prevented the product from achieving perfection. "Perfection" denotes flawlessness or excellence in nature. It is impossible for the seed of Adam to achieve this. An imperfect product cannot create a perfect system of government. Prov. 14:12 best described this impossible task: "There is a way which seems right to a man and appears straight before him, but at the end of it is the way of death." A perfect union denotes that all citizens have access to all benefits equally. A government system whereby a small percentage of the population controls the majority of the wealth does not reflect perfection. The Manufacturer and His plans and purposes are perfect. The only way the product can come near perfection is through and by Him.

Perfection is a process in which maturity is the objective. Even if the product had the ability within himself to be perfect, it would require being developed. Because of the statement of "to form a more perfect Union," the consensus of the citizens of the United States was that perfection was already established and there was no need to develop. To add salt to the wound, religion gave her approval, and the Church remained silent. Everyone bought into the ideal of a more perfect union. Again, perfection leaves no room for further improvement. The problem with this whole concept is that the product does not have the ability within himself to carry it out. To compound matters, the founders were contaminated with a virus of superiority that expanded to such a degree that citizens of a particular ethnic group or gender were seen as an inferior and perceived to have been created for the sole purpose of serving the superior group. Perfection does not lend itself to superiority and inferiority, as all are created equal.

The establishment of justice requires total commitment, which must be connected to discipline, integrity, and accountability. Success in implementing the amendments of the Constitution was predicated on individuals whose hearts were pure. The product cannot purify its heart. The heart can only be made pure by divine intervention. When the "authority of the people" takes priority over the principles of the Manufacturer, divine intervention will not take place. It is impossible for a law promulgated by the product to produce justice when the authors demonstrated a lack of impartiality. Again, the product is flawed; and therefore, a flawed product cannot produce justice. Justice requires knowledge of Truth. Truth cannot be released without a connection to the Manufacturer. Without Truth, the product is like a dog chasing its tail. The objective will never be met.

Justice is a trait of righteousness and impartiality. This comes from the heart and cannot be provided by the product. Impartiality comes out of a heart free of contamination. The product is not in a position to bring righteousness to himself. Righteousness denotes right standing with the Manufacturer, but the fall of Adam resulted in this unrighteous status.

Insuring domestic tranquility places a demand on those responsible for the value of tranquility for all citizens. Tranquility is related to peace, and peace denotes freedom from opposition. Tranquility cannot be achieved without divine intervention. Peace is a trait of the Manufacturer, and He, and He, only determines where it lands. The tranquility of the product is limited to the natural realm. The product is a spirit that resides in a body, and has a soul. So, if tranquility is maximized, it will impact only two-thirds of the product.

Providing "for the common defense, promoting the general welfare, and securing the blessings of liberty" requires discipline, integrity, and commitment. It is not just saying the words that bring productivity; it is a commitment to executing the law for all citizens. The founders sought to create a utopian environment, but this ambitious undertaking could not be achieved by the product. Promoting the general welfare is a commendable desire, but the attitude of the product would not lend itself toward unity. The head was in the right place, but the heart was corrupted. Head commitment without integrity of the heart is like a hurricane of monumental proportions destroying everything in its way. When the heart of a nation is derived from religion, destruction is expected. When the heart is corrupt, division and deception take root, and potential is aborted.

Chapter Five

The Constitution— The Potenial of a Nation

The new nation was influenced by ideas and beliefs expanded from the European caste system. The expansion entailed, in a subtle way, ethnic purity.[26] The hand of the caste system shaped the nation's ideas concerning slavery and equality for all, including the equality of women, since it appeared that equality was limited to the white male.[27] What happened to the inalienable rights of life, liberty, and the pursuit of happiness for all citizens? (The realization of this statement would require an extreme conscience effort.)

The Constitution gave the nation the potential to become a land that was for all people. Its words echoed the heart of the Manufacturer. But again, words without substance and execution are just words. The Constitution could never live up to the expectations of those who wrote it because the commitment required to uphold it to its fullest was not in their hearts. The founders were not able to do this because they did not have the heart of the Manufacturer.

Freedom of speech was established under Amendment I of The Constitution. However, today, under the guise of the 1st Amendment, civility has been removed altogether. Radio and television personalities can load the air waves with venom, attacking those who do not agree with their opinions, and their words are applauded by those who do. Many of these personalities hide behind their freedom of speech, when, in fact, the directive given to those that aligned themselves with the Creator is clear and precise: "Let your conversation be always with grace, seasoned with salt, that ye may know how ye ought

---

26 Roark et al, p. 298; Divine et al, p. 474
27 Roark et al, p. 225

to answer every man," (Colossians 4:6). "A gentle tongue [with its healing power] is a tree of life, but willful contrariness in it breaks down the spirit," (Proverbs 15:4). "He who guards his mouth and his tongue keeps himself from troubles," (Proverbs 21:23). These scriptures give us the superior plan for proper communication. In essence, the First Amendment lowers the communication standards because the standard reflects the morals of the person and the nation.

The First Amendment guarantees freedom of speech, but it does nothing to insure integrity and truth. It offers the opportunity to exploit the truth in the name of freedom of speech, suggesting that the opinion of the one communicating is more valuable than truth. Remember, a lie can be accepted to such extent that it takes on its own life. The force of the lie is then so powerful that it gradually changes the terrain and landscape. This change has a permanent impact on the environment, such that it is now polluted with darkness, and the magnitude of that darkness cannot be measured by the product. The morals of this nation were such that many were willing to fight to preserve the status quo, as evidenced by the Civil War.

Truth and justice were not factors in the decision to fight. The war was driven by morals of the nation. The questions that must be asked are: Was the North driven into this war because of their dislike for slavery or was it based on economics? Was it possible that the Northern states were envious of the Southern states, since the southern states had a built-in source of revenue: cotton, tobacco, cash crops and the cheap labor of slavery? To a large degree, this environment was, for the south, a "promised land." The land flowed with milk and honey; the honey was the crops, and the milk was the slaves. While the southern states took the position that emancipation would mean economic collapse and social anarchy, the North's position was that emancipation would benefit the country economically.

Regardless of the reasons for war, both sides shared the common belief, and that was the slave was inferior to the master; after all, the northern states had slaves at one time also. In the scheme of things, there was not much difference between the two. Although historians seek to paint a different picture. Former Alabama Governor, George C. Wallace stated in the 1968 Presidential campaign, "There isn't ten cents' worth of difference [between them])."[28] He was referring to the Democrats and the Republicans, but the same could have been said of the North and South in reference to their commitment to the equality and equal protection under the law for slaves.

Many have used the same landscape that was reshaped by lies and given creditability by religion as a means of spewing out their vain opinions, preconceived ideas, and bigotry. When religion is connected with democracy, each party has a measure of believability. This enabled the founders to carve on the canvas of history the notion that this marriage of religion and democracy was sanctioned by the Manufacturer. Thus, lies became truth, truth became lies, and confusion ran rampant. In reality, the product became the victim of its own deception, which further destabilized a system that was already on unstable ground. Thus, the latter stage became worse than the first stage.

The vast majority of the product remained captivated by the system, and could not recognize the danger. Business continued as usual, wrong became right, and no one dared to challenge the status quo, especially since it had the approval of the religious system. The First Amendment became a gospel in itself. This was an insult to the Manufacturer because it draws more attention to the product than to the Manufacturer. As a result, the Constitution has become a graven image. The Bible is clear as recorded in Exodus 20: 3-5, "You shall have no other gods before or besides me. You shall not make yourself any graven image [to worship it] or any likeness of anything that is in the heavens above, or that is in the earth beneath, or

---

28 Carter, p. 334

that is in the water under the earth. You shall not bow down yourself to them or serve them; for I the Lord your God am a jealous God, visiting the iniquity of the fathers upon children to the third and fourth generation of those that hate me."

The focus shifted from the works of the Manufacturer to the works of the product. It is a bold attempt by the product to establish parity with the Manufacturer. Anything that projects the product as equal to the Manufacturer is out of order. This gives the enemy the opportunity to exercise two of his modes of operation: the lust of the eye and the pride of life. These traits of the power of darkness change the focus; thus, the product has a desire to maintain some level of glory. This position takes an opposite view of the principles expressed by the Manufacturer.

As with the product's attempt in the building of the Tower of Babel (Genesis 11), the intent of the founders was also motivated by pride. The Constitution could not be a finished product. It was a work in progress. The consensus is that it was a completed product; therefore, it has creditability. Man cannot create a system of government that is above reproach. In Mark 7: 21-23 it states, "For from within, [that is] out of the hearts of men, come base and wicked thoughts, sexual immorality, stealing, murder, adultery, converting (a greedy desire to have more wealth) dangerous and destructive wickedness, deceit; unrestrained (indecent) conduct; an evil eye (envy), slander, (evil speaking, malicious misrepresentation, abusiveness), pride (the sin of an uplifted heart against God and man), foolishness (folly, lack of sense, recklessness, thoughtlessness). All these evil [purposes and desires] come from within, and they make the man unclean and rendered him unhallowed."

The Constitution and Declaration of Independence are commendable documents. The founders were courageous in creating them, but a deficit occurred when it came to implementation. It takes a more ardent endeavor of devotion to execute the plan than to establish the plan. This has been the case as it relates to all the Constitutional Amendments. The laws are passed by Congress, but states and the local government must enforce them. The questions to ask are: Do the states have the same zeal as the federal government? Will the federal government place a demand on the states to enforce the laws that they promulgated? If there is a deficit in the chain of command, responsibility, accountability, and discipline will never take place. It was a lack of responsibility that cost the lives of thousands in the Civil War and initially denied women the right to vote.

The laws were passed, but little or no demand was placed on the leaders to fairly enforce them. To a large degree, the state and local government knew the consequences of their actions, and because the heart was corrupt, responsibility took a back seat. Hypocrisy existed in the federal government, also, because the federal government could place the responsibility at the state and local level, and keep their hands clean.

The best example of this is the northern and southern states' stance on voting. The southern states had legal barriers that maintained segregation and prevented the former slaves from voting. The Southern states also used gerrymandering.[29] The result remained the same, minimizing the ability of those wanting to participate in the process. The hypocrisy came forth during the Reconstruction Period, after the Civil War, when the carpetbaggers exploited those they were sent to help. This hypocrisy remained intact during and after the Civil rights Movement. The south inflicted Black Codes (1865-1866) and Jim Crow laws (1865-1965).[30] However, the North had a credibility issue too. Whereas, in the South, you could see the product's contaminated heart, in the North, although the fruit looked good on the outside, the heart was contaminated on the inside. (The North was segregated in the areas of housing, marriage, adoption, education and employment.) Two evils were

---

29   Roark et at, p.394-398; Divine et al, p. 475-477
30   Franklin and Moss, p. 238 and p. 436-470

opposing each other while wrapping themselves around the flag of patriotism.

Patriotism does not mean righteousness. Righteousness is superior to patriotism. Yet, in today's society, patriotism has been elevated above righteousness. The radio and television talk shows place more emphasis on patriotism than on the principles of the Manufacturer. It appears that patriotism and religion have signed a pact. Religion has given her support to patriotism, and patriotism to religion. However, there is a vital piece of the puzzle that is missing, and that is Truth. Unfortunately, the meal of patriotism and religion has added another course: liberals and conservatives.

Religion embraces an ideal that the status quo is ordained by the Manufacturer. Its stamp of approval gives legitimacy to the conservative's position. Conservatism and Liberalism, within themselves, are neither positive nor negative. However, failing to recognize Truth give access to deception. Thus, Truth is not placed in high esteem by either one, and this missing link continues to keep both sides out of the realm of light. Pro-life is a position taken by most, if not all, conservatives. It is a courageous stand. However, it is not limited to the child in the womb, but must remain the objective after the child is born. Every spirit sent to earth surrounded by a body has potential, purpose and destiny. To abort means that potential has been abandoned, purpose is forfeited, and destiny cannot be reached. The original intent of the Manufacturer is altered by the product, either while the child is in the womb or after the child is born.

Remember, if the heart is corrupt, it is impossible for the product to produce righteous traits. Therefore, righteousness has to come from the Manufacturer. The prophet Isaiah described the condition of the product in Isaiah 64:6, "For we have all become like one who is unclean [ceremonially, like a leper, and all our righteousness (our best deeds of rightness and justice) is like filthy rags or a polluted garment; we all fade like a leaf, and our iniquities, like the wind, take us away [far from God's favor, hurrying us toward destruction]." No matter what conservatives or liberals say, the product is not capable of making righteous decisions disconnected from the Source.

One's political ideology does not make one right with the Manufacturer. Many conservatives have sought to make this case but the Manufacturer is neither liberal nor conservative. He is righteous and self-sufficient. He is neither a Democrat nor a Republican, nor is He the author of democracy. He is a theocrat, and His system is theocracy. The success of the product in producing laws to benefit all is predicated on the Product being connected to the Manufacturer. The product cannot improve on the principles of the Manufacturer. Remember, the product was created in His image; the Manufacturer was not created in the image of the product. This speaks volumes about the attitude of the product throughout the history of this nation, proclaiming justice and equality, while being moved by a corrupt heart in enforcing the laws. The measure of a nation is not in what the nation says; it is in what a nation does.

The first paragraph in the Declaration of Independence is a profound statement. It states, "When in the course of human events, it becomes necessary for one people to dissolve the political bands which have connected them with another, and to assume, among the powers of the earth, the separate and equal station to which the laws of nature and of nature's God entitle them, a decent respect to the opinions of mankind requires that they should declare the causes which impel them to the separation." Being separated from the mother country did not change the condition of the heart. The same spirit of injustice that ruled the mother country ruled the new nation. This spirit was fueled by the spirit of religion, and religion has left its fingerprint on all.

The founders had the opportunity to place the Words of the Manufacturer above their laws, because His thoughts and words are superior to the words of the product (Isaiah 55:8). It is hypocritical to say you that believe in a source greater than yourself, and yet place your opinions above His principles. The founders chose to be driven by the concept of "the authority of the people." Failing to make Him Lord created creditability problems for the founders, which began as a small seed, but has produced a great harvest. This nation has placed a greater emphasis on the words of the founders than on the words of the Manufacturer. What a loss of potential.

Chapter Six
The Absence of Truth

Pilate asked Jesus, "What is truth?" (John 18:38). Centuries later we are still asking that question. In essence, an absence of Truth has always been the issue in religion. Truth denotes the reality that lies at the core of the matter. Truth stands on its own; it makes one free. Truth goes beyond the opinion of the liberals as well as the conservatives. It goes beyond the opinion of the media, the Tea Party, the National Association of the Advancement of Colored People (N.A.A.C.P), Daughters of the Confederacy, and any other organization. Truth takes priority over the doctrine of the Southern Baptist, Baptist, Methodist, African Methodist Episcopal (A.M.E.) Church and all other denominations. Truth takes priority over Catholicism, Protestantism, Buddhism, Islam, Hinduism, and all other religions. Each of these has its own agenda, yet none is above reproach, and none has full access to Truth. As popular as conservatives and liberal talk shows are, they do not represent Truth. There will always be an audience eager to accept their opinions and influence; but, again, their opinions and influence do not express the Truth, because Truth is not determined by the opinions of the majority. Truth stands on its own. And when Truth is not present, darkness has total control.

The lack of Truth has always divided this nation. The divide existed long before the Civil War. It existed before the writing of The Constitution. It existed before the Pilgrims arrived. The lack of Truth resulted in the divide between the Catholics and Protestants, which goes back to the causes of the Protestant Reformation.[31] Each group was seeking supremacy at the expense of Truth. Jesus came to restore, while an aspect of the product sought to divide. What was absent from their pool of information was

---
31 Ferguson and Bruun, p. 356-369

Truth. An abandonment of Truth was recorded in every culture, generation, and ethnicity. The product became eloquent in expressing his opinion and in establishing rules and laws, but foolish in identifying Truth and therefore, unable to live together in peace. As a result, the freedoms detailed in the Constitution have pitted young against old, rich against poor, Republicans against Democrats, management against workers, as each feels he or she has the rights to exercise their convictions, because each believes Truth is on his side.

Building a nation on an inferior foundation inevitably leads to destruction. A nation or a group within a nation seeking to devalue the product that was made in the image and likeness of the Manufacturer is the highest form of disrespect. It is fueled by pride and a desire to perpetuate self. It is an indication that those buying into this belief have been blinded and have no knowledge of Truth. As it has been stated before, the Trinity walks in total unity and everything the Manufacturer created is a reflection of Himself. Every spirit He sent to earth surrounded by a body is valuable. Each was redeemed by the same precious blood of the Son. The act of Adam placed every product in the same position to be influenced by sin. The blood of the Son placed everyone who believes in Him in the position to be influenced by righteousness. Everyone shares the common bond that all have missed the mark, and none are able to reconnect to the Manufacturer without direct intervention from Him. Romans 5:8-9 says, "But God shows and clearly proves His [own] love for us by the fact that while we were still sinners, Christ (the Messiah, the Anointed One) died for us. Therefore, since we are now justified (acquitted, made righteous, and brought into right relationship with God) by Christ's blood, how much more [certain is it that] we shall be saved by Him from the indignation and wrath of God."

The scripture does not say that one ethnic group was above sin while the others were polluted by sin. It says that since all are in the same category, all suffer from the same illness. Neither the purest of blood, the highest level of education, nor greatest wealth can remove the stain of this illness. There is only one kind of blood that can address the illness of sin. According to 1 Peter 1:19-20, "But [you were purchased] with the precious blood of Christ (the Messiah), like that of a [sacrificial] lamb without blemish or spot. It is true that He was chosen and foreordained (destined and foreknown for it) before the foundation of the world, but He was brought out to public view (made manifest) in these last days (at the end of the times) for the sake of you."

In Isaiah 1:4, the prophet revealed the heart of a nation that rebels against the Manufacturer: "Ah, sinful nation, a people loaded with guilt, a brood of evildoers, children given to corruption! They have forsaken the Lord; they have spurned the Holy One of Israel and turned their backs on Him." In verse six he writes, "From the sole of the foot even to the head there is no soundness or health in [the nation's body] -- but wounds and bruises and fresh and bleeding stripes; they have not been pressed out and closed up or bound up or softened with. [No one has troubled to see a remedy.]"

The arrogance of a nation that proclaims its allegiance to the Manufacturer while rejecting Truth is reprehensible. The nation of Israel suffered the devastating consequences of their sins. They were exiled to Babylon (Jeremiah 50:17). The action against Israel was sufficient evidence that all nations must comply with the Word or suffer the result of rejecting the Word. This nation is no exception. The founders had access to the writings of the Prophet Isaiah but refused to see the benefits of obeying the Word.

Throughout this nation on any given Sunday, the churches are filled with individuals zealously singing and giving praises to the Manufacturer, but without knowledge and Truth. This is the concept upon which this nation was established - acknowledging Him, but choosing the "authority of the people." The "authority of the people" missed the mark because the heart of the people determines their actions. If the heart is established on religious ideas, the actions and words will reflect those ideas. Again, it is evident that religion has failed the product. Remember, religion is the product's means of reconnecting to the Manufacturer.

Religion, to a large degree, supports the concept of the "authority of the people." In this system, the people bring their religious ideas and beliefs to the table; however, just as you cannot separate the water from the wet, you cannot separate people from their religion. While the First Amendment prohibits any law concerning the establishment of religion, the fact remains that the individuals who create the laws are motivated by their religious beliefs. Every man involved in creating the Constitution was driven, to a degree, by his religious background. Whatever we are taught lies below the threshold of our consciousness. A child is not born with hatred toward another person. It is taught. Where one's affection lies, the heart will follow. Religion can express greed, racism, sexism, intolerance, prejudice, and still maintain its credibility.

One of the strongest requirements of religion is that works must be done by an individual to demonstrate his goodness. The heart can be corrupt as long as the works are pleasing. But the reality is that the works cannot be pleasing when the Word is rejected. The Word takes priority over the works. When the product places more value on his principles than on the Word, he is saying that the Word is insignificant.

The Constitution, Bill of Rights, and the Declaration of Independence are examples of works. It is not that these documents are evil in themselves, but placing them above the principles of the Manufacturer is a form of idolatry. It is a matter of giving His glory to another, or substituting something or someone in His place. The prophet Isaiah expressed the heart of the Manufacturer in sharing His glory. As Isaiah 42:8 says, "I am the Lord; that is My name! And My glory I will not give to another, nor My praise to graven images." If this is a Christian nation, then the principles of the

Manufacturer would take priority over documents of the product. The product would pay homage to Him and not to the works of his own hands.

A major tragedy in this is the unwillingness of the Church, in general, to stand up for Truth. It has become a church with no backbone, comprised by religious ideas, honoring the praise of the product over the directive of the Manufacturer. Because light is absent, both political parties are victimized by individuals with personal agendas. Each is influenced by the religious right as well as the left. However, Truth is absent in both cases. It appears the Conservative right controls the Republican Party, while a segment of the Liberal left controls of the Democratic Party. The result of these two extremes is that Truth and light have no access. Both sides are influenced by zealots without spiritual knowledge, who worship their own ideas or the ideas of the founders.

The true measure of a Godly nation is its knowledge of and intimacy with the Person of Jesus Christ. Paul expressed it this way in Philippians 3:10: "[For my determined purpose is] that I may know Him [that I may progressively become more deeply and intimately acquainted with Him, perceiving and recognizing and understanding the wonders of His person more strongly and more clearly], and that I may in that same way come to know the power overflowing from His resurrection [which it exerts over believers], and that I may so share His sufferings as to be continually transformed [in spirit into His likeness even] to His death..."

This kind of relationship far exceeds the best the product can offer. Thus, He becomes the objective and the focus of the nation, as well as of individuals. The opinions of the product are controlled by His Words, Truth, and righteousness. The product surrenders his will to the will of the Manufacturer and is no longer in competition with the Manufacturer. A relationship is established, and the product receives the Manufacturer as his or her Father. The dynamics have changed. There is a shift from religious ideas to a personal relationship. Remember, religion acknowledges that He exists; but, relationship makes the product one with the Manufacturer. The Manufacturer's desire since He created Adam and Eve has been a relationship. The best the product can produce will always fall short of this goal. The guidelines must be established by the Superior and not the inferior.

The essence of Truth cannot be determined by the product, and the product cannot comprehend its value. A lack of Truth will negatively impact everyone. Regardless of ethnicity or skin color, all have the same corrupt heart. If the power structure was controlled by all learned folk void of Truth, the result is the same. It does not matter the class or the intellect, if Truth is missing, chaos, destruction, and bondage will eventually manifest. Again, the writer of Proverbs 16:25 expressed it well, "There is a way that seems right to a man and appears straight before him, but at the end of it is the way of death."

Because of a lack of knowledge, many have placed the division in the nation on racism, sexism, and class. However, the real villain is the absence of Truth, and this affects all ethnicities. The deception is that the product has the answer to all of humanity's challenges. Because Truth is absent, the product is blind and controlled by facts accumulated by the product. The result is that the product sees things through the vision of the world, and not through eyes of Truth.

Chapter Seven

The Truth Will Make Us Free

When the product seeks to bypass the Son, the relationship is broken. The product is at the mercy of his own skill and knowledge. The product is playing the game with several disadvantages: the eyes of the product are blinded; the ears cannot hear, and there is no foresight. A nation that takes this position reflects the heart of those without perspective. Remember, each seed produces after its kind; therefore, a seed without vision produces a harvest without vision. A seed without knowledge produces a harvest without knowledge. It is not the opinions of the majority that produce Truth. Truth produces truth. The majority can be deceived just as an individual can be. Unfortunately, this mindset in which the majority is accepted as the only source of Truth is a perilous path. The concept of "majority rule" lends itself to the notion that there is something intuitive in the thinking of the "majority" that makes it superior. In the modern understanding, majority rule suggests truth inferred from plurality, or something that is fixed in the mind of many.

When determining truth or trying to find truth, every action of the product, such as the Declaration of Independence, Bill of Rights, and Constitution, falls short of the goal. Over a period of time, the cracks in these documents have been exposed. Democracy is not complete. It is only a beginning that has to be fine-tuned. The cracks stem from the fact that the founders thought it was a completed concept. As a result of that lack of knowledge, no one sought to address the fact that it is unable to back up its own words and live up to its potential. On paper, it looks good, it feels good, it has the support of the majority, but no one has an understanding of how to implement the rules so that everyone benefits. From an external view, democracy is the best thing since sliced bread; but, internally there are major flaws. The focus has been on the external, while being oblivious to the internal. And therein lies the problem. All the great leaders of this nation focus on the positive while ignoring the negative.

History is the number one witness against this nation, and its testimony is sufficient to warrant an indictment. The witnesses for Truth have declared in Psalms 85:11, "Truth shall spring up from the earth, and righteousness shall look from heaven." This statement speaks volumes about the value and the creditability of Truth. Unfortunately, the "authority of the people" was chosen over Truth, and this choice has great consequences. The product continues to glory in his authority while being blinded to the result. Each generation has the responsibility to make the right choice because Truth is still knocking at the door. As the "authority of the people" continues to perpetuate self, Truth becomes less important. Thus, each generation that rejects Truth adds its name to the list of those who prevent justice and righteousness from taking their proper place.

Joshua had to make a decision, as recorded in Joshua 24:15, "And if it seems evil to you to serve the Lord, choose for yourselves this day whom you will serve, whether the gods which your fathers served on the other side of the River, or the gods of the Amorites, in whose land you dwell; but as for me and my house, we will serve the Lord." The bold statement, "But as for me and my house, we will serve the Lord" speaks volumes about making a righteous decision. The founders had a choice to make. They could either continue the pattern of the European community and the caste system, or choose the principles of the Manufacturer. Their choice was to maintain the same pattern as the European community, a pattern which was rooted and grounded in the bowels of religion. In embracing the "authority of the people," the founders made a decision based on tradition and not on Truth.

The evidence is clear that Truth was neither then, nor is it now, the objective of the nation's leaders and a significant segment of the Church. The notion that the Constitution was ordained by the Manufacturer, and that it was complete indicates a lack of knowledge. Completeness is only established by the one that knows the purpose of a thing or a person. Completeness requires one to establish the end before the product is created, and to know the correct function of the product. Completeness considers all aspects of that which has been created, and addresses its totality.

If the Constitution was completed and ratified in 1788,[32] why was there need for the Thirteenth, Fourteenth, Fifteenth, and Nineteenth Amendments (or any of the amendments, for that matter)? Clearly, the Constitution was a starting point, not a finished product. It was an earnest attempt by a flawed product to achieve success based on the ability of the product. It has fallen short of its goal because the laws and rules were executed by the same flawed individuals. It is impossible for the thing that is crooked to make itself straight. The thing that is polluted cannot make itself pure. The Civil War is a prime example of the stubbornness of individuals who refused to accept Truth, and for whom the status quo was more important.

The tragedy is that neither the Church, the nation nor religious leaders have learned from this calamity. The divide continues to grow between the rich and poor, between the educated and uneducated, and between the many ethnic groups. The political and religious arenas provide the fuel that sparks these divides, while the Church seeks to display a position that is pleasing to all sides. This absence of light has created an environment that has placed the nation in danger. This has happened because there is no voice of Truth that takes a stand against this poison of compromise. The reason is that the Constitution takes precedence over the Word; but, the Word has a specific standard as noted in Colossians. 4:6,"Let your conversation be always full of grace, seasoned with salt, so that you may know how to answer everyone."

---

32 Roark et al, p. 187

As a citizen from heaven sent to earth to represent the superior Government, the Christian must express the teachings and the principles of the superior Government. The First Amendment places great emphasis on the powers of Congress; however, the powers of Congress must also submit to the principles of the superior Kingdom. This means the laws promulgated by Congress must reflect the principles of the Manufacturer, and the Person of the principles. The person that confesses his or her Christianity must remain dedicated to their conviction at all times. In this relationship, the product does not have an option, because of the laws and rules of the product. The laws and rules of the product must reflect the principles of the Manufacturer. Christianity requires one to be a doer of the Word, and not just a hearer of the Word. James 1:25 says, "But he who looks carefully into the faultless law, the [law] of liberty, and is faithful to it and perseveres in looking into it, being not a heedless listener who forgets but an active doer [who obeys], he shall be blessed in his doing (his life of obedience)."

The Declaration of Independence, Bill of Rights, and Constitution all consists of words; however, Christianity is a lifestyle that rises above the product's words. Jesus said, "…The words I have spoken to you are spirit and they are life" (John 6:363 NIV). His Words must remain above everything that is done. His Word remains steadfast, as stated in, Psalms 119:89: "Forever, O Lord, Your Word is settled in heaven." Since His Word is superior, the words of the product must be inferior; therefore, greater emphasis must be placed on His Words. His Words require the product to abide in them, and His Words must abide in the product. Abiding in His Words and His Words abiding in the product brings Him glory (John 15:7-8).

Placing greater emphasis on the ideas, rules, and laws of the product over those of the Manufacturer is a step in the direction of idolatry. The word idolatry is defined as: "a blind or excessive devotion to something."[33] When the Constitution becomes the object of devotion and allegiance, in the

---

33   American Heritage College Dictionary, p. 675

eyes of the Manufacturer, the army of idolatry is marching forward. Where the seeds of idolatry have been sown, a harvest is inevitable. Galatians 6:8 states, "For he who sows to his own flesh (lower nature, sensuality) will from them reap decay and ruin and destruction, but he who sows to the Spirit will from the Spirit reap eternal life." The reaping is a process, but it is certain.

The bottom-line is all of the systems of government adopted by the product are flawed. The truest form of a righteous government is the government of the superior Kingdom. The prophet Isaiah received knowledge concerning this system of government in Isaiah 9:7: "Of the increase of His government and of peace there shall be no end, upon the throne of David and over his kingdom, to establish it and to uphold it with justice and with righteousness from the [latter] time forth, even forevermore. The zeal of the Lord of hosts will perform this." Notice, this system of government is forever and is established upon justice and righteousness. It does not need the approval of Congress, the President, or any action by the product.

Majority rule cannot prevent a nation, state, or community from perishing. Remember, the majority that rules is part of the human race, and has inherited the sins of the first product, Adam. The great deception lies in the notion that the majority brings Truth to the table. It does not. Truth takes precedence over the opinions of the majority, and it must rule with impunity. Only with Truth and mercy will iniquity be removed. Proverbs 16:6 states, "By mercy and truth iniquity is purged: and by the fear of the Lord men depart from evil." This scripture tells us that evil is not removed by the actions of the majority. Evil is actually removed when Truth runs like a mighty river and righteousness like a stream. It seems the founders were moved to believe that a majority opinion would automatically prove to be an opinion that would benefit all; consequently, any opposing view is considered anti-American.

Freedom that a country can provide is grossly over-emphasized. The product, as previously stated, is a spirit that resides in a body and has a soul. The laws promulgated by the product fail to address the needs of the spirit man. They do not have the power to do so. These needs can only be addressed by the Manufacturer. Therefore, this is another example where religion sought to accomplish something outside its territory and failed. While freedom of speech is applauded by the product, the Manufacturer's principles are established on a more solid foundation. His principles far exceed freedom of speech. His principles place great emphasis on accountability, because words produce either life or death. Proverbs 18:21 states, "Death and life are in the power of the tongue, and they who indulge in shall eat the fruit of it [for death or life]." Freedom of speech without accountability breeds chaos.

Confessing Christianity as a way of life places a demand on each citizen who embraces this truth to allow the Manufacturer to control what they say. What one says is a measure of one's commitment. Commitment must extend its wings to reach all aspects of the Word. When commitment limits itself, the end result is inadequate. Thus, the whole is seen as being defiled and lacking creditability, which causes many to question the validity of the nation's Christian values. Corrupt communication has produced a spirit whereby the product worships the creature more than the Creator (Manufacturer).

The Church is the source of light. Jesus made this clear in Matthew 5:14, "You are the light of the world. A city that set on a hill cannot be hidden." When light exists, it cannot be hidden. Where light is absent, darkness prevails. The light the Church has been assigned to produce for the world is not in the opinions, concepts, and doctrines of the product. Light can only come from the Source that created it. The opinions of the product can never reach the level of light and truth that comes from the Source of Truth. It is not within the DNA of the product to produce a system that addresses the needs of the spirit and the soul. This ability is reserved for the Manufacturer. Seeking to do so places the product outside the realm of his ability. After all, knowing and abiding by the Truth will make us free (John 8:32).

Chapter Eight
The Iniquity of a Nation

Truth took a backseat because the source of light, the Church, was so connected to the status quo that she refused to produce light. In the absence of light, bias, greed, and jealousy rule without any opposition. Bias produces its own gospel with its own version of creation, all the while abandoning Truth and its principles. In this version, creation was a two-stage event, in which the superior group was created first, followed by the creation of the servant group. Under this concept, it is easy to understand why the product believed they were aligned with the desires of the Creator, despite the fact that there was no evidence to support their position. Their position was the result of a twisted mind motivated by a corrupt heart.

Psalms 51:5 states, "Behold, I was brought forth in [a state of] iniquity; my mother was sinful who conceived me [and I too am sinful]." According to Matthew 24:12, "And the love of the great body of people will grow cold because of the multiplied lawlessness and iniquity." Iniquity is one thing that the oppressed and the oppressor have in common. Iniquity has ruled with impunity, while love has steadily declined. Iniquity impacts every ethnic group, male and female, rich and poor, educated and uneducated, pastors and parishioners, politicians and constituents, and young and old. Iniquity establishes a false reality that places the product in an environment whereby Truth cannot be recognized; thus the "authority of the people" becomes the reality. Iniquity is so rooted and grounded in the product that darkness is seen as light, lies become truth, death is as life, and zeal takes priority over knowledge.

All of the words of the product, as decreed in the Bill of Rights, Declaration of Independence and Constitution carried little or no weight since there was no commitment to honor them. This lack of commitment reveals the heart of the product, while the Manufacturer places great value on His Words, Psalms 119: 89, "Forever, O Lord, Your Word is settled in heaven [stands firm as the heavens]." The writer in Psalms 138:2 goes to another level in expressing the value of His Word: "I will worship toward Your holy temple and praise Your name for Your loving-kindness and for Your truth and faithfulness; for You have exalted above all else Your name and Your Word and You have magnified Your Word above all Your name!"

Because iniquity is driving the product, there is no means of moving away from the traits of iniquity. As long as iniquity is in control, the product is at its mercy. In reality, the product's thoughts, opinions, and rules are shaped by iniquity. Proverbs 14:12 bears repeating: "There is a way which seems right to a man and appears straight before him, but at the end of it is the way of death." The power of iniquity is that it creates an environment in which the product is not able to distinguish a lie from the truth, darkness from light, and death from life. What seems right has the support of the people and is accepted as being above reproach.

The Constitution, Bill of Rights, and Declaration of Independence were written over two hundred years ago. Yet, if we are truthful, we must acknowledge that the implementation of them has been flawed. These flaws have been exposed throughout the history of the nation. Therefore, one must inquire, when these documents were written, what was really in the hearts of the founders? What were their objectives, and how did they plan to achieve them? Since the founders are dead, the answers to these questions have to lie in the result – the government based on the "authority of the people" does not work for all of the people, but for a specific group.

Again, the opinion of the majority is not the measure for success. President Lincoln's statement, "…government of the people, by the people, for the people, shall not perish from the earth,"[34] speaks more about the ability of the product than to their allegiance to the Manufacturer. President Lincoln failed to consider the power of iniquity. The presence of iniquity draws the product away from the Manufacturer. This places the product in a no-win position where protection from the onslaught enemy is not available. Psalm 6:8 says, "Depart from me, all you workers of iniquity, for the Lord has heard the voice of my weeping." The Manufacturer has no connection with workers of iniquity, and as long as iniquity abounds, the product is in a hopeless state. The product continues to do the same thing, but expect a different result. Unless iniquity is removed the result will always be the same.

According to Isaiah 53:5, "… He was wounded for our transgressions, He was bruised for our guilt and iniquities; the chastisement [needful to obtain] peace and well-being for us was upon Him, and with the stripes [that wounded] Him we are healed and made whole." The product had no solution for his transgressions, or for his iniquities, and neither did religion. The "He" that is mentioned is the only One qualified to remove iniquity. He is the Son. Hebrews 2:14-15 says, "Since, therefore, [these His] children share in flesh and blood [in the physical nature of human beings], he [Himself] in a similar manner partook of the same [nature], that by [going through] death He might bring to nought and make of no affect him who had the power of death- that is, the devil- And also that He might deliver and completely set free all those who through the [haunting] fear of death were held in bondage throughout the whole course of their lives."

While the power of iniquity has been removed through the finished work of the Son, the product has the responsibility of accepting this finished work. The opportunity is available because Jesus has declared His position and provided access to the Father (Manufacturer) through the Son, giving the product the opportunity for sonship, according to John 1:12, "But to as many as did receive and welcome Him, He gave authority (power,

---

34 Divine et al, p. 415

privilege, right) to become the children of God, that is, to those who believe in (adhere to, trust in, and rely on) His name." The Manufacturer is now Father and has given His sons and daughters victory through the work of the older Son.

Christianity goes beyond the limitations of religion. The very definition of a Christian denotes confessing a belief in Jesus as the Christ and the Son of God. Christianity is about a relationship based on kinship, consummated by the death (blood), burial, and resurrection of Jesus Christ. One of the strongest attributes of the Father that He demonstrated by sending His Son, is love. Love does not discriminate, show partiality, or seeks its own way. According to 1 Corinthians 13:4-7, "Love endures long and is patient and kind; love never is envious nor boils over with jealousy, is not boastful or vainglorious, does not display itself haughtily. It is not conceited (arrogant and inflated with pride); it is not rude (unmannerly) and does not act unbecomingly. Love (God's love in us) does not insist on its own rights or its own way, for is not self-seeking, it is not touchy or fretful or resentful; it takes no account of the evil done to it, [it pays no attention to a suffered wrong]. It does not rejoice at injustice and unrighteousness, but rejoices when right and truth prevail. Love bears up under anything and everything that comes, is ever ready to believe the best of every person, its hopes are fadeless under all circumstances, and it endures everything [without weakening]."

This kind of love has not often been expressed in this country. Love makes no decision to place certain individuals in bondage because of their lack of education or wealth, their gender, or the color of their skin. This kind of love would never have embraced slavery and discrimination, considered a Civil War pitting brother against brother, or allowed segregation, Jim Crow, or the Ku Klux Klan to rule with impunity. This kind of love would have ensured that justice and equality were made available for all. The Father's love was released on all of mankind, not just on a certain ethnicity. John

3:16 gives clarity: "For God so greatly loved and dearly prized the world that He [even] gave up His only begotten (unique) Son, so that whoever believes in (trusts in, clings to, relies on) Him shall not perish (come to destruction, be lost) but have eternal (everlasting) life."

This truth of love presented a great challenge for the founders because of their commitment to the "authority of the people," which consisted of the religious ideas of the people. Each founder came to the table with religious ideas, and those ideas took priority over the teaching of the Lord Jesus Christ. The beginning of the Preamble of the Constitution states, "We the people of the United States, in Order to form a more perfect Union…" If this is a Christian nation, then, "We the people" should actually reflect on the wisdom and leadership of the Manufacturer.

King Solomon sought wisdom from the Manufacturer, as recorded in 2 Chronicles 1:9-10, "Now, O Lord God, let Your promise to David my father be fulfilled, for you have made me king over a people like the dust of the earth in multitude. Give me now wisdom and knowledge to go out and come in before this people, for who can rule this Your people who are so great?" Solomon knew the task at hand was too great for him. The reply from the Manufacturer in verse 12 was that, "Wisdom and knowledge are granted you. And I will give you riches, possessions, honor, and glory, such as none of the kings had before you, and none after you shall have their equal."

The Bible tells us that we have not because we refuse to ask (James 4:2). Any group seeking to establish a nation without seeking advice from the Manufacturer does not value His wisdom and knowledge. Therefore, one can suppose, if He is not considered valuable, He does not have proper access. This action proves that the nation is not "one nation under God," as expressed in the Pledge of Allegiance.

The Manufacturer expects and encourages the product to seek Him, as we see in Psalm 53:2: "God looked down from heaven upon the children of men to see if there were any who understood, who sought (inquired after and desperately required) God." Instead, the product rejected truth and, therefore, became a slave to lies. This action takes issue with Psalm 119:105: "Your Word is a lamp to my feet and a light to my path." His Word cannot be compromised (Psalm 119:89). His Words takes precedence over everything. His Words are superior to the best that the Product can offer. His Words give light that removes all forms of darkness.

The product sees the Manufacturer through the eyes of religion. Religion sees the Manufacturer as ruling; however, the product has the option of either accepting or rejecting Him. This lies below the threshold of the product's consciousness. Neither the product nor the founders would ever acknowledge it, but their actions revealed what was in their hearts. It also reveals that religion has a greater influence over this nation that the Word or the Person of the Word.

Making the Word of no affect is not a new phenomenon. An inferior mindset will always seek to reduce the significance of that which is superior. The inferior mindset is controlled and dominated by pride. In essence, pride is the god of this mindset, and darkness is its son. This mindset uses extreme measures to protect its territory. This mindset is as a virus causing destruction throughout the nation. It has not been exposed because, within the deception, Truth has been overlooked.

With the concept of "one nation under God," instilled in the Pledge of Allegiance, one must inquire, what God are we talking about? The god of religion, or the God of Truth? Maybe it is the god of democracy, or the god of the people, after all, the people are in control. Maybe it is the god of greed, or of racism? The God of this nation needs to be established and qualified. The true God is the Self-Sufficient One, the Creator, the Provider, and the Protector. In Exodus 20:2-3, He describes Himself: "I am the Lord your God, Who has brought you out of the land of Egypt, out of the house of bondage. You shall have no other gods before or besides Me." He goes on to say in verse 6 that He shows, "...mercy and steadfast love to a thousand generations of those who love Me and keep My commandments."

Relationship with the Manufacturer differs from religion in that He shows mercy and steadfastness to a thousand generations; whereas religion cannot provide mercy or love (religion does not even address one's needs). The Manufacturer provides grace and Truth through His Son. John 1:14 says, "And the Word (Christ) became flesh (human, incarnate) and tabernacled (fixed His tent of flesh, lived awhile) among us; and we [actually] saw His glory (His honor, His majesty), such glory as an only begotten son receives from his father, full of grace (favor, loving-kindness) and truth." This grace is birthed out of a relationship that religion cannot provide.

Relationship says that the Superior One values the inferior one and views the inferior one as worth redeeming, despite his flaws. This is not predicated on the behavior or works of product, but on what the Superior One sees and on what He has placed in the product. Thus, this relationship has less to do with doing, and is fundamentally about being. The "doing" of the product could never reach the level whereby the sin issue could be addressed. The "being" is a process whereby the superior blood of Jesus Christ has removed the contamination of sin, and the product has been restored back to the days before the fall of Adam.

In this, the product's words should express the heart of the Manufacturer. The Words of the Son produce life, so the words of the product must do likewise. Words spoken by the product that generate death do not represent the One that produces life. Words that demean other ethnic groups do not reflect the heart of the Son, or the Manufacturer. Words that depict others as sub-human are the product of the darkness personified.

This level of darkness challenges the integrity, credibility, and completeness of the Manufacturer. Remember, He said, Let us make man (mankind) in our image. No group has a corner on truth, purity, or innocence, for all have fallen short and sinned (Romans 3:23). With this information, how can any group see itself as being above reproach? This could only be achieved through a distorted view of the truth, in which the views of the product took precedence over the Truth of the Manufacturer. Consequently, the founders made a decision to maintain their position, to guard and protect it with a rigid code of ethics. This was allowed because Truth was prevented from taking its rightful place in their hearts. Remember, intimacy with Truth is the only means by which freedom is obtained. Antagonism towards Truth has produced a harvest of falsehood not easily recognized. It produces culture and class wars, racism, and sexism.

The Civil War was a catastrophic event in our nation's history, and the residual effects remain. At that time, it was the North against the South; today it is the Liberals against the Conservatives, the Democrats against the Republicans, and the rich against the poor, and the educated against the uneducated. The enemy's objective remains the same - to kill steal, and to destroy (John 10:10). The great disappointment is that the nation's spiritual and political leaders have not learned the lesson from the Civil War. Many opportunities were missed because the greater emphasis was placed on the ideas of the product than on the principles of the Manufacturer.

The status quo was accepted without opposition, despite information that it presented an opposing view to that of the Manufacturer. The Apostle Paul expressed it this way in 2 Corinthians 4:3-4: "But even if our Gospel (the glad tidings) also be hidden (obscured and cover up with a veil that hinders the knowledge of God), it is hidden [only] to those who are perishing and obscured [only] to those who are spiritually dying and veiled [only] to those who are lost. For the god of this world has blinded the unbelievers' minds [that they should not discern the truth], preventing them from seeing the illuminating light of the Gospel of the glory of Christ (the Messiah), Who is the Image and Likeness of God."

The actions of the founders were predicated on the opinions of the majority rather than on the knowledge of the Manufacturer. This was due to pride, wrapped in self-reliance, and it is the true essence of darkness. Isaiah 14: 13-14 says, "And you said in your heart, I will ascend to heaven, I will exalt my throne above the stars of God; I will sit upon the mount of the assembly in the uttermost north, I will ascend above the heights of the clouds; I will make myself like the Most High." The founders followed this same pattern, but their iniquity was the abandonment of Truth.

Chapter Nine

Repentance— A Nation's Challenge

Every worthwhile cause demands work. The words listed in the Declaration of Independence are incredible in nature; however, words without work are irrelevant. If this nation is to live out its mandate, its leaders must work together to ensure that the laws are executed properly. The same intensity that was used to write the Constitution, Declaration of Independence and Bill of Rights must be used to make sure the words of these documents are fairly implemented. Thus, the nation and every believer must learn that the only way this can happen is through a connection to the Source, Jesus Christ.

Unfortunately, the challenge with this nation is that she has sought to maintain the concept of democracy, while failing to recognize that only the Manufacturer knows the way His creation is designed to function. Proverbs 3:5-6 says, "Lean on, trust in, and be confident in the Lord with all your heart and mind and do not rely on your own insight or understanding. In all your ways, know, recognize, and acknowledge Him, and He will direct and make straight and plain your paths."

King Solomon expressed it well in Ecclesiastes 12:13 when he said, "Let us hear the conclusion of the whole matter: Fear God, and keep His commandments: for this is the whole duty of man." The Manufacturer has placed a demand on Himself to place His Word above His Name. In turn, the product must place a demand on himself to fulfill his duty by keeping the Manufacturer's commandments. This requires maintaining a personal relationship with Jesus Christ and growing in the knowledge of His truth and righteousness. It also requires all who believe in Him to be individuals of godly character, integrity, and accountability.

"The authority of the people" was weak on work because the consensus was that the Declaration of Independence, Bill of Rights, and Constitution were finished works. They were not, because additional Amendments were required. These additions were not an acknowledgment of failure; but, they did reveal the incompleteness of the foundational documents that existed from the outset. The Manufacturer makes known the end from the beginning (Isaiah 46:10). He takes into consideration every possible event, situation and circumstance. Nothing surprises Him. He is prepared for all. Hence, if He was the author of these documents, there would not be a need for any adjustments. He never starts something that He has not finished.

If the product identifies with the Manufacturer, His ways must become the product's ways. The life and light in the Son enables the product to show love for the Manufacturer. Since the Manufacturer does not show partiality, the product is bound to follow this same pattern. When the product refuses to walk in love, light is not in him. 1 John 2:9 says, "Whoever says he is in the Light and [yet] hates his brother [Christian, born-again child of God his Father] is in darkness even until now." Verse 11 continues: "But he who hates (detests, despises) his brother [in Christ] is in darkness and walking (living) in the dark; he is straying and does not perceive or know where he is going, because the darkness has blinded his eyes." No nation, community or individual can say they are walking in love when there is abhorrence for another because of their color, ethnicity, culture, financial, or educational status.

Again, this appears to be is a reflection of the caste system that had a stronghold in Europe. It is obvious that knowledge of the Manufacturer has been missing. The product has had a zeal for Him, but zeal must be married to knowledge. This lack of knowledge has prevented the nation from addressing major problems that were lying below the surface. Rights for all citizens should have been a priority, especially when the leaders inserted "In God We Trust" on the currency and "…one nation under God…" in the Pledge of Allegiance.

When Have We Walked TOGETHER?

The God of all creation has a plan and purpose for everything that He created, including the creature made in His image and after His likeness. Since He has a purpose for each, the country that proclaims her allegiance to Him must see the value of each person. The necessity of the 13th, 14th, 15th, and 19th Constitutional Amendments suggests the founders did not see the total picture as it related to all individuals. And because of this, the oppressors are locked into the notion that they are superior to others, while the oppressed are locked into the notion that they are inferior. Each fails to see as the Manufacturer sees. Ironically, the oppressors and the oppressed are both in bondage, and neither recognizes their condition.

Every athlete, no matter what sport, knows the value of training. Great athletes anticipate the attributes of their opponents, and know how to neutralize them. As with great athletes, great leaders know the value of their plans and how to execute them. They also know that for every great plan there will be great opposition. However, despite the opposition, there has to be a predetermination to stay the course and execute the laws fairly and justly for all. The predetermination has to be so deeply rooted and grounded that nothing will bring about a compromise.

If this was the case, then how determined were the founders to be men of their words? The Declaration of Independence clearly states, "All men all created equal, that they are endowed by their Creator (the Manufacturer)..." Were their words meaningful, full of integrity, and intended for all, or were they merely providing a lip service without the substance to back up their words? If this is the case, then "all" does not mean all, but only a selected group.

Matthew 15:8 says, "These people draw near Me with their mouth and honor Me with their lips, but their hearts hold off and are far away from Me." This scripture is basically saying that the heart is lukewarm because it has never really connected to the Source. Without the Manufacturer, the heart is filled with deadly poison that contaminates and perverts. In this state, the heart has become so asphyxiated that no effort of the product can provide what is needed. The oxygen of truth is no longer available; therefore, the product cannot be revived in its present state. The product must seek help from the Source who created Him. If he doesn't, he continues to dwell in his abyss.

The natural man is so deeply rooted in darkness that his conscience is not subject to Truth. He can't discern it even when Truth is revealed to him. From the outset, the product's corrupt heart has prevented him from seeing through the eyes of Truth. The notion that another member of the human race could determine the value of others is foolish thinking. And because this concept was not challenged at the outset, it has grown and produced a harvest of other equally distasteful ideas and hypocrisy.

Post-Civil War Reconstruction sought to address the legal grievances of the ex-slaves. The 13th Amendment was ratified in 1865; however, after the assassination President Abraham Lincoln, it needed additional Constitutional support, so the 14th Amendment was ratified in 1868. However, it appeared that the ratification of the 14th Amendment had more to do with increasing the power of the Republican Party than removing the obstacles for ex-slaves; therefore, 15th Amendment was ratified in 1870.[35] Although, these Amendments were recorded on books, little was done to implement or enforce them.

A major reason for this was the federal government refused to use its power to demand that southern states comply with the law. These Amendments were promulgated for the benefits of the slaves, but others used these laws for their own benefits. In many cases, these laws were used to protect businesses, and large corporations. The 14th Amendment, though it granted citizenship to the newly freed men, was used to protect and maintain segregation, thus, the lack of enforcement denied the freed men equal protection.[36]

35 Boyer et al, p. 525
36 Roark et al, p. 396-397

When Have We Walked TOGETHER?

Due to a lack of enforcement, the 15th Amendment, granting the right to vote to the freed men, did little to remove the stigma of former slaves as second-class citizens. It did little to protect the former slaves from their ex-masters or bring about any form of justice for the former slaves, because the ways of the nation had not truly changed. The nation's leaders failed to honor their own words. It was of political expediency to pass these amendments, but it appears there was little or no commitment to enforce them. Again, this was the greatest form of hypocrisy. And this hypocrisy is still with us today.

This hypocrisy has remained primarily because of an absence of individuals willing to place Truth over tradition and religion. Religion and tradition have been the cornerstones of the nation that few dare to challenge either for fear they would be labeled as unpatriotic or, worse, enemies of the Constitution. Greater fear is exhibited toward being accepted by others than fear and reverence toward the Manufacturer. Jesus expressed this in John 12:43, "For they loved the praise of men more the praise of God." The Manufacturer does not approve of laws that force the product to abort his or her assignment in the earth or of opinions and ideas that do not represent His principles. God created all, and He has an assignment for all. As long as the focus is on the product, the principles of the Manufacturer will be missed. Humanity has failed to grasp that a disconnection from the Source is a disconnection from Truth, righteousness, wisdom, knowledge, and understanding.

When the soul of a man is controlled, influenced, and dominated by a corrupt heart, negative results are inevitable. This nation has accomplished much; but many of the accomplishments were external. Jesus expressed it this way in Matthew 23:25-27 "You clean the outside of the cup and dish, but inside they are full of greed and self-indulgence. Blind Pharisee! First clean the inside of the cup and dish, and then the outside also will be clean. Woe to you, teachers of the law and Pharisees, you hypocrites! You are like whitewashed tombs, which look beautiful on the outside but on the inside are full of dead men's bones and everything unclean."

For example, the election of President Barack Obama suggested to the world that the nation had reached a stage where skin color is insignificant, where each person is judged by the content of their heart and character, and where all have access to all the benefits. This is not the case. Rather, the election of President Obama only revealed the venom of hatred and racism lying beneath the surface.

Being conservative is not equivalent to having a relationship with the Source of life. It simply means one adopts a conservative view. The great tragedy is that the Church has refused to shine light on the subject. As a result, many have removed the value of the One who redeemed the product and emphasize conservative values over the Word. Thus, conservative ideas are given priority over the Lord Jesus Christ; but conservative views cannot remove the stain of sin or make one right with the Manufacturer.

The political views of the product, whether liberal or conservative, cannot atone for sin. The sin which separated the product from the Manufacturer can only be addressed by the Manufacturer. The Bible is clear in Acts 4:12 [Leadership Bible]: "Salvation is found in no one else, for there is no other name under heaven given to men by which we must be saved." Both Conservatives and Liberals present some good ideas; however, their ideas and opinions cannot produce salvation. Each presents some level of knowledge, but only the Son brings knowledge, life and Truth. Each has many supporters, but numbers in themselves do not establish truth.

In a sense, the political system has brought much affliction on the nation, because greater emphasis is placed on this system than on Truth. The system of democracy has its limits, and neither party acknowledges those limitations. Therefore, as candidates campaign for a particular office, their platforms have very little to do with Truth. It's unfortunate that it appears their objectives are to expose the flaws of their opponents. In many cases, the personal agendas of the candidate take priority over those being represented. Thus, the good of the people is ignored. This system, in which the nation places all of its confidence, is one in which many of the elected officials fail to understand the value of accountability. It is obvious that the system needs a major overhaul, yet no one is willing to challenge it.

One cannot declare "In God We Trust" or that we are "one nation under God" only when it is convenient. There is no Christianity without adhering to His principles, because His principles take priority over "the authority of the people." There is no Christianity without the Lord Jesus. His principles require that each believer comply, and compliance brings obedience. Thus, the qualification for being a Christian is not based on race, gender, religion, or political affiliation. It is based on those that put their trust and confidence in the finished work of the Son. This is in direct opposition to the principles of this world's system. The world's system places greater emphasis on the opinions and the desires of the product than on principles of Manufacturer.

The nation has to surrender her ideas and opinions so that the principles of the Manufacturer become the number one priority. Had this been the case from the beginning, it would have changed the perspective, and Truth would have prevailed over lies, light over darkness, and life over death. It is so unfortunate that religion has played a vital role in shaping the nation's personality, culture, and objectives, because the opinions of the majority have been shaped by their religious views. James 1:15 says, "Then the evil desire, when it has conceived, gives birth to sin, and sin, when it is fully matured, brings forth death." When sin is in operation, it brings forth death.

To prevent this death, repentance is required. Repentance is an acknowledgement that wrong has occurred, and the one that committed the wrong is Godly sorry for missing the mark. It is obvious that the nation's founders and leaders have missed the mark. The mark was missed from the beginning, during the writing of the foundational documents. It was missed prior to the Civil War, and up to the present time. Yet, at no time has it been recorded that the nation's leaders called for repentance? It appears not, because it is the consensus of nation's leadership and, unfortunately, even the Church that no evil was committed; therefore, no repentance is required. And this mindset has driven the nation, as well as the Church, away from repentance.

This mindset has taken root in the hearts and the minds of leaders to such a degree the value of the principles of the Manufacturer have taken a back seat to the ideas and opinions of the product. While the principles of the Manufacturer are being scrutinized by all religions, the ideas and opinions of the product remain above reproach. This is no coincidence, because the power of darkness seeks to keep the product focused on self. Therefore, the Truth of the Word will not bring conviction. This explains why generation after generation continues to follow this same pattern. To a large degree, the mindset of the Church is the same as that of the nation. But, the responsibility of the Church is greater than that of the nation. As a matter of fact, the Church has the responsibility of providing Godly leadership by example.

The Manufacturer always provides an opportunity for repentance. 1 John 1:9 states, "If we freely admit that we have sinned and confess our sins, he is faithful and just true to his own nature and promises and will forgive." Recognizing sin is required in order to repent from sin. Failing to recognize sin gives sin the opportunity to reign in other areas. The scripture states, we must confess the sin. To confess is to acknowledge that we have missed the mark. Repentance is required for the many lives that were lost during the Civil War, for all those who potentials were aborted as a result of the enforced Black Codes and Jim Crow laws, for every individual who was denied the right to life, liberty and the pursuit of happiness as depicted in the Constitution, but even more significantly as mandated by the Manufacturer.

It could be said that the measure of a country's strength is its Gross National Product (GNP). I say the measure of a country's spiritual development is the level of trust it places in the Manufacturer. This determines a country's strength. As a nation, the challenge for growth in the right direction is to repent of our sins.

Chapter Ten
The Iniquity of the Church

The spiritual death of the nation came as a result of the spiritual death of the Church. Jesus referred to the Church in Matthew 5:13-14 as the salt of the earth: "You [church] are the salt of the earth, but if salt has lost its taste [its strength], its quality, how can its saltiness be restored? It is not good for anything any longer but to be thrown out and trodden underfoot by men. You are the light of the world. A city set on a hill cannot be hidden." Salt preserves. Salt keeps things from spoiling or rotting; therefore, without salt, what was designed for good will spoil and decay. The nation's foundational documents were designed for good; but in the end, without the salt, they were destined to decay. The product could not justly implement them, because the product needed the Manufacturer to do this.

The voice designed to bring Truth into its proper position remains absent. That voice belongs to the Church. The Church has been reluctant to take a Godly stand as it relates to justice and equality for all races and creeds. The Church has been reluctant to make sure the second paragraph of the Declaration of Independence takes the position "that certain unalienable rights avail themselves to all citizens" is implemented to its fullest intent.

The Church has been given the assignment of expressing Truth in the earth. The Truth from the Manufacturer far exceeds that of the product. Therefore, if Truth is to abide in the earth, the Church must walk in Truth. The Great Commission, as revealed in Mark 16:15, stresses the preaching of the gospel, which reveals the heart of the Manufacturer. Since the gospel is ordained of Him, the gospel is the Truth. It is the responsibility of the Church to reveal this truth.

The Church has a mandate from the Head of the Church to proclaim that it was His blood that redeemed the product. Thus, the greater indictment is on the Church and her leadership for failing to proclaim the Word. The Church has failed to recognize and execute the power and authority she has been given. This has placed her in a position of following instead of leading. She is illuminated by the principles of the world instead of illuminating the world with light from the principles of the Manufacturer. She has been captivated by the belief that the hand of the Manufacturer (God) is all over the nation's foundational documents, justifying her from acting upon the principles of the Word. As a result, many generations have bought into this lie, and the lie has produced a stronghold of eminent proportions. The level of this stronghold is so rooted and grounded in the hearts of a significant number of church leaders that they prefer popularity over light and Truth. In doing so, many have surrendered their responsibilities to the government, making the government the product's provider, lord, and savior.

Because the Church failed as an outlet of Truth, the infrastructure on which this nation was established is compromised. Truth kept warning the product that there were consequences for his actions. Yet, because the product, encouraged by a segment of the Church, placed greater emphasis on religion, Truth was forced to take a backseat. When Truth took a backseat, darkness and deception ruled with impunity. Instead of dismantling erroneous information, the erroneous information was perpetuated, causing every generation to be impacted. And instead of the Church setting the example, the Church allowed religion or the "authority of the people" to be the example.

Throughout the history of this nation, from its inception and all the events since then, one must inquire, where was the Church? Where was the Church when it came to implementing justice and equality for all? Where was the Church when it came to providing for the poor? Where was the Church when it came to showing the love of God when division in the nation brought on the Civil War? What was the Church's stance on the war? Did the Church pray or fast prior to the war? During the war, did the leaders pray for divine intervention, or for unification that would benefit all mankind, instead of a select few? Perhaps, if the Church was in her rightful place, there would not be a need for these questions, because, Truth would have been able to exercise its authority. The nation would have benefited greatly, and history would have been rewritten. Equality for all would have reigned throughout the land.

Hosea 4:6 it states, "My people are destroyed for lack of knowledge; because you [the priestly nation] have rejected knowledge, I will also reject you that you shall be no priest to Me; seeing you have forgotten the law of your God, I will also forget your children." The great emphasis is placed on the spiritual leadership (the priests, pastors). When there is an absence of true Church leadership, neither light nor knowledge is manifested. Thus, the subsequent generations are shut out and kept in the dark concerning His principles and His truth. This lockout opened the door to the greatest form of spiritual violence which impacts every aspect of the product's life.

One must be mindful that the devastation caused by the war was not limited to the more than six- hundred thousand lives lost. It does not include the aftermath of destruction that plagued the nation spiritually, mentally, and physically. There are wounds that still exist to this day as a result of the Civil War. Creation itself is still crying out for the manifestation of the Sons of God (Romans 8:19). Just as the blood of Abel cried out from the ground when he was killed by his brother Cain (Genesis 4:10), the blood of those soldiers continues to express its displeasure.

The outcome of the war did little to bring unity and resolution of the many challenges the nation faced. (Besides the cost in human lives, many cities were devastated, not to mention the financial cost of the war for both sides). Establishing unity required more than removing the chains of slavery for the more than four million ex-slaves that required immediate attention. In addition, reconstruction and reunification were challenges that needed divine intervention immediately. Without divine intervention through prayer, it was impossible to reach an agreement and understanding on these issues. And yet, the driving force behind the chaos was still the "the authority of people."

President Lincoln's quest for reunification was to be commended; however his original intent exposes his true commitment to the process. Wendell Phillips, an abolitionist from Boston, charged that the President "makes the negro's freedom a mere sham."[37] Basically, he was saying the President, following the original pattern, removed the commitment so that the laws and rules were circumvented. When you remove a tiger's teeth, his bite becomes ineffective. This was the case with the President's plan for unification. In his Proclamation of Amnesty and Reconstruction, the President provided full pardon to those willing to renounce secession and accept the abolition of slavery. This proclamation provided for the restoring of all property and full political rights; however, it did not address the needs of the four million former slaves (It seemed that the objective of the President was geared more toward unification rather than dealing with the issue of the freed slaves.) In his inaugural address, President Lincoln was steadfast in his efforts by declaring, "let us strive on to finish the work we are in; to bind up the nation's wounds…to do all which may achieve and cherish a just, and lasting peace."[38] What the President failed to understand was that such a peace could not be achieved by the product, because the product needed divine intervention. It needed the Church to pray. Sadly, instead of praying, the Church took a backseat

The enormous challenges the nation faced placed the nation in a position whereby seeking divine intervention should have been the response. The

---

[37] Roark et al, p. 389
[38] Roark et al, p. 389

"authority of the people" could not provide what was needed. Yet it maintained its position and actually gained strength and popularity, while seeking divine intervention was viewed as an option, and not a need. This has been the pattern from the outset, and the Civil War is one of the results of that pattern. This pattern shows an unwillingness to address the wrongs of the nation. Despite the thousands of deaths, loss of resources, and division in the nation, the "authority of the people" remained the focal point. Jesus expressed His heart on this matter in Mark 7: 8-9: "You have let go the commands of God and are holding on to the traditions of men, And He said to them; You have a fine way of setting aside the commands of God in order to observe your own traditions!"

This focus continued to prevail, despite the assassination of President Lincoln. In his eagerness to restore relations with the Southern states, Lincoln's successor, President Andrew Johnson, also failed to take into consideration the needs of the former slaves. To a large degree things remained as they were. This played into the hands of southerners who had been clearly defeated, but not subdued. [39]

While leading the nation at its most critical time in history, there was a lack of spiritual knowledge and a failure to repent for the sin of slavery. President Johnson failed to assert the needed leadership. 1 John 1:9-10 states, "If we [freely] admit that we have sinned and confess our sins, He is faithful and just (true to His own nature and promises) and will forgive our sins [dismiss our lawlessness] and [continuously] clean us from all unrighteousness [everything not in conformity to His will in purpose, thought, and action]. If we say [claim] we have not sinned, we contradict His Word and make Him out to be false and a liar, and His Word is not in us [the divine message of the Gospel is not in our hearts."

---

39   Franklin and Moss, p. 206-207; Divine et al, p. 454-458; Boyer et al, p. 517-521; Roark et al, 394-398

These scriptures bring an indictment against the nation. Sadly, few church leaders were bold enough to acknowledge the sins of the nation. To say that one has not sinned is making the Manufacturer into a liar. And, if the Manufacturer is a liar, the Gospel is not the Truth, and everyone is still in sin. It clearly states in Titus 1:2 that the Manufacturer cannot lie: "In hope of eternal life, which God, that cannot lie promised before the world began." Furthermore, Hebrews 6:17-18 states, "Accordingly God also, in His desire to show more convincingly and beyond doubt to those who were to inherit the promise the unchangeableness of His purpose and plan, intervened (mediated) with an oath. This was so that, by two unchangeable things [His promise and His oath] in which it is impossible for God ever to prove false or deceive us, we who have fled [to Him] for refuge might have mighty indwelling strength and strong encouragement to grasp and hold fast the hope appointed for us and set before [us]."

Since the Father will never be proven false, the falsehood lies in the product. One of the best examples of falsehood in the nation is religious men seeking to circumvent their own laws as occurred after the Civil War. Many southern states, with the approval of the President and the Congress, enacted a series of laws known as the Black Codes. These laws made emancipation a travesty, because the slaves were not really free. The action, or lack thereof, by the federal government in allowing these laws to exist is beyond one's comprehension. Obviously there was no fear, reverence or respect for the principles of the Manufacturer, or for the Person of the principles because everyone, including the Church, yielded to the "authority of the people."

The fact that greater emphasis was placed on the product than on the Manufacturer has given access to every evil spirit. This nation continues to suffer today from these acts of evil. Deuteronomy 28:15 says, "But if you will not obey the voice of the Lord your God, being watchful to do all His commandments and His statutes which I command you this day, then all these curses shall come upon you and overtake you." This environment existed because the pastors (shepherds) neglected their responsibilities by not declaring the Word. Some even modified the Word for their own benefit. Obeying the voice of the Lord requires one to hear His voice, and in hearing His voice, a demand is placed on each hearer to obey His voice.

Failing to do what one has been instructed to do is disobedience. Placing the desires of the product over the principles of the Manufacturer puts the product in a helpless position that is intensified because of the proud nature of the product. This pride has blinded the product from the Truth, and the Gospel is hidden from him. 2 Corinthians 4:3 says, "For the god of this world has blinded the unbelievers' minds [that they should not discern the truth], preventing them from seeing the illuminating light of the Gospel of the glory of Christ (the Messiah), Who is the Image and Likeness of God." The blindness has caused the product to believe his opinions have parity with the Manufacturer's principles; therefore he believes that he has an option to choose either the principles of the Manufacturer or his own ideas.

The immediate aftermath of the Civil War indicates that no reverence was shown for the superior knowledge of the Manufacturer, and little or no respect was displayed for His principles. The northern states retreated from a commitment to justice and equality for all, while the southern states swore to save southern civilization from a descent into African barbarism and black rule. The corruption of the two-party system permitted this to go on while the Church remained indifferent, refusing to produce light. The evil was so strong and contagious that one person is recorded to have said, "We must render this either a white man's government, or convert the land into a Negro man's cemetery."[40] It is reprehensible that a nation that had suffered the loss of so many lives would speak with such contempt and show complete disregard for humanity.

The lack of the Church's input and involvement allowed darkness to

---

40   Roark et al, p. 407

establish itself without any opposition. The Church was mandated to let the light shine in Matthew 5:16: "Let your light so shine before men that they may see your moral excellence and your praiseworthy, noble, and good deeds and recognize and honor and praise and glorify your Father Who is in heaven." Shining the light exposes the darkness, and light reveals the love of the Father and the excellence of His name. Light also exposes the inferior thinking of the product while revealing the superior thinking of the Manufacturer. Thus, the Church is mandated to think like the Head and not submit to the ideas of the people.

History reveals that the aftermath of the Civil War left many unresolved issues. Enforcing the Constitution remained inconsistent. Creditability and integrity were mere words without substance, like clouds producing no rain. Yet, the leaders on both sides remained adamant in protecting their traditions, favoring them over Truth. Righteous solutions maintained their distance, while confusion and chaos took their place. Thus, the failure lies with the Church.

The environment of this nation at that particular time was the same as some third world countries today. Violence was as American as apple pie, and few wanted to acknowledge it. The Democratic Party of the southern states turned to terrorism. Night riders were released on the ex-slaves and white sympathizers.[41] These individuals accomplished their mission and ruled with impunity. Greed and self-righteousness, which added to the violence, wreaked havoc over the nation. Neither the oppressors nor the oppressed realized they were being used by a force whose power far exceeded theirs. Because of their blindness, they each blamed the other for their circumstances. Each failed to recognize that in order to amend the circumstances, a connection with the power higher than the enemy was required, and this power is the Lord Jesus Christ.

---

41   Franklin and Moss, p. 226-227; Roark et al, p. 406-407; Boyer et al, p. 529-530; Divine et al, p. 467)

Unfortunately, one-hundred-thirty years later, this lesson is still not learned. The same groups continue to blame each other. As long as this attitude remains, the country will always be divided, because no one group is above reproach and no one has the solutions within themselves. The Manufacturer does not love one group more than another. This lie must be exposed and destroyed. Joel 2:28 states, "...I will pour out My Spirit on all people]. Your sons and daughters will prophesy, your old men will dream dreams, your young men will see visions." He does not say that He will pour His Spirit on some, but on all. This means that everyone has access to His Spirit, His righteousness, His truth, His forgiveness, His peace, and His love. I John 4:10 puts everything in perspective: "In this is love; not that we loved God, but that He loved us and sent His Son to be the propitiation (the atoning sacrifice) for our sins."

As the country moved forward, the effects of the sins of the past continued to grow. Without confessing the sin, the sin remains alive. The only means by which sin can be removed is when it is confessed. Only then is the sin covered by blood of the Second Person of the Godhead. One of the negative traits of this country has been an unwillingness to acknowledge its sin (Isaiah 14:13-14). This unwillingness is the product of pride, and pride is the strongest characteristic of the power of darkness. The power of darkness was removed from his position because of pride. With pride and self-righteousness, the product will always have a mindset whereby the focus is on him and his ideas. Under these conditions, seeing and recognizing truth is outside the realm of his ability.

History reveals that the source of light, the Church, failed in its assignment; therefore, the nation was deceived into believing it was without sin. The Church, as well as a nation that maintain its wholeness will see no reason to repent. This was, and is, the iniquity of the Church.

Chapter Eleven
The Great Commission

The Great Commission is the last recorded instruction in the Bible of Jesus to all of His followers. Mark 16:15 states, "And He said to them, go into all the word and preach and publish openly the good news (the Gospel) to every creature [of the whole human race]." The Good News informs the product that he can be restored back to the Manufacturer. The Good News is made available to all ethnic groups. The Good News means that the product is not only restored, but that he is in the same position as Adam before the fall. The Good News declares that the Son is the mediator between the Manufacturer and the product, and that everyone has access to Him. The Good News provides the means whereby the product, through Jesus Christ, can walk in dominion. This level of dominion includes things in the spiritual realm as well as things on the earth. This level of dominion requires that the product maintains a constant relationship with the Son.

The Great Commission requires Godly leadership. It requires individuals willing to stand in the gap for a people and a nation, proclaiming the Gospel, without comprising the principles of the Manufacturer. Thus, the Great Commission requires true leaders. A true leader must be able to govern himself with the highest form of integrity, courage, and commitment to purpose, understanding that his responsibility is for the good of all, regardless of how it is perceived by the masses. Therefore, a true leader is able to turn adversity into opportunity, while maintaining control in an adverse environment.

The Son is a true leader. The Son knew the awesome responsibility He was given by the Manufacturer. He knew that the cost of dying on the cross and being separated from the Manufacturer was great. Although He knew that He was without sin, because of the love for the product, He endured the cross, despised the shame, focused on the joy that was set before Him (Isaiah 53:5). Outweighing the temporary unpleasantness, He did what He was sent to Earth to do. He knew that the awesome rewards would come with a great price, but in the end it was worth it. True leadership is not fulfilled when the followers are not inspired to release their full potential. As with the Son, true leaders must abandon the comfort zone and even see it as an enemy. The enormous responsibility placed on the nation before and after the Civil War demanded true leaders.

Leadership also requires the ability to follow. In fact, at one time, a leader had to be a follower in order to learn how to lead effectively. A leader must see opportunity, potential and purpose in everyone. This removes any and all desires to place one group over another group, because a true leader wants justice and equality for all, as declared in the Constitution. A true leader desires that all benefit and have access. A true leader recognizes that when even one person is in bondage, all are in bondage.

Leadership requires strength, integrity, discipline, and patience. According to Proverbs 16:32, "He that is slow to anger is better than the mighty; and he that rules his spirit, than he that takes a city." These traits are required in order to execute laws fairly and with justice. The need for discipline is essential in leading and inspiring others. Those who choose to remain in their comfort zones do not provide Godly leadership. Comfort zone players will not make unpopular and righteous decisions. Those decisions require discipline and dedication, which they do not possess.

While justice remained adrift for minorities, women, and the poor, those in authority continued their blind leadership. (Thus, the Carpetbaggers of the North and the Klan of the South wreaked havoc on the ex-slaves and those sympathetic to their cause. The leadership of the nation was so infected with the virus of hatred that the Klan ruled with a level of impunity, and the

Carpetbaggers exploited the situation for their own benefits. Both groups disguised themselves as angels of light when, in fact, they were wolves in sheep clothing. Ironically, each group had the support of a segment of the Church, and this is what brought creditability to their positions. In many ways, the Klan was an extension of the church. Many ministers, lay persons and deacons worked faithfully in the church on Sunday while lynching ex-slaves Monday through Saturday.) This was done in the name of the Lord, in an effort to protect the superior Caucasian race from the inferior black race. (Women, as well, as the poor were also seen as inferior to the superior Caucasian male.)

The tragedy is that all were victimized. Those in power saw themselves through the eyes of pride and considered themselves above reproach. Many of the oppressed saw themselves as inferior and accepted this as their lots in life. Although many ethnic males saw themselves as superior to females, it appeared that they considered themselves subservient to Caucasian males. However, the fact that laws are not being implemented fairly does not excuse failing, or not accepting responsibility for one's own actions. The oppressed have access to Truth from the Manufacturer, and the focus must be on the Manufacturer's promises. When the oppressed abide by the principles of the Manufacturer, equality, justice, and freedom derives from within, regardless of what the oppressors say.

The mentality of many in this nation is that if the Manufacturer's hand is on the works of the founders, such as the foundational documents, He has approved everything the founders have declared. This does not agree with the Word, as revealed in Jeremiah 17:5-6: "Thus says the Lord: Cursed [with great evil] is the strong man who trusts in and relies on frail man, making weak [human] flesh his arm, and whose mind and heart turn aside from the Lord. For he shall be like a shrub or a person naked and destitute in the desert; and he shall not see any good come, but shall dwell in the parched places in the wilderness, in an uninhabited salt land."

The potential for the product's success is predicated not only knowing the principles of the Manufacturer, but by abiding in the Son. He said that without Him, the product can do nothing (John 15:5). In other words, the product can do nothing to remove the stain of sin. Within himself, the product cannot produce a service that will bring pleasure to the Manufacturer, and he cannot produce laws that are pleasing to the Manufacturer. Whenever the product seeks to be productive, he drifts from the Manufacturer, and his work is fruitless and worthless. In the end, his work will eventually be destroyed. However, when the heart of the product abides in Him and is united in Him, then his productivity is unlimited. The product is then in a position whereby he can ask what he will, and it shall be done (John 15:16).

Religion does not give the product this level of access to the Son, because religion is not about relationship. Abiding in Him means that the product has a personal relationship with Him, which gives the product access to the principles, promises, and the Person of Jesus Christ. Remember, all the promises of God are in Him, [Christ]. 2 Corinthians 1:20 states, "For as many as are the promises of God, they all find their Yes [answer] in Him [Christ]. For this reason we also utter the Amen (so be it) to God through Him [in His Person and by His agency] to the glory of God."

The Church is not a part of this world system, nor is the Church a part of an earthly nation. Her allegiance is not to anyone or any group – not the democrats, republicans, or to democracy. Her allegiance is to the Kingdom that the Church represents. The Church cannot serve two masters, because seeking to serve the government of the product and the Manufacturer will lead to confusion. Serving the government of the world results in total destruction and frustration. Serving the Manufacturer restores order and corrects vision.

Religion rejects the only Source that can provide the relationship with the Manufacturer, thereby forfeiting all of the promises made by the Manufacturer. In a subtle way this concept was released at the onset of the country. "We hold these truths to be self-evident, that all men are created equal; that they are endowed by their Creator with certain inalienable rights; that among these are life, liberty, and the pursuit of happiness." "All men" denotes all humanity – all of the descendants of Adam– on every social and economic level, and every ethnic group. Religion has been used to support the belief of some that their ethnicity, education, and morality make them superior to others. The practices of the nation must reflect the Lord Jesus Christ.

The enemy of Light and life continues his rampage through the opinions expressed based on the "authority of the people." It was stated earlier that since the heart of humanity is corrupt, the opinions express the condition of the heart. A corrupt heart cannot see the value in others; consequently, others are viewed as inferior and less than human. This attitude drives the opinions of the "authority of people." Because of the corruption of the heart, which is the objective of sin, the product is intuitively elevating itself while demeaning others.

This suggests that the product has chosen his own way and has rejected Truth. It says that the product has established his own principles, and that he expects the Manufacturer to certify or approve them. Where was it ever recorded that President Lincoln stated the Manufacturer's views on the evil act of slavery? The product fails to comprehend that the Manufacturer confirms His words, not the opinions of the product.

Truth and light must be released by the Source of light and Truth, not by the product. When the product is pursuing his own goals, perpetuating his own desires, and seeking his own glory, Truth cannot be recognized. Truth is discovered by connecting and maintaining that connection to the Source.

Abiding in Him is the requirement by which Truth is released. John 8:32 says, "And you will know the Truth, and the Truth will set you free." Truth takes priority over the facts, opinions, and ideas established, held and developed by the product. Without Truth, everything that the product touches becomes toxic. What many consider the product's best- democracy, for example, is rooted and grounded in the same toxic foundation.

The challenge is that the product does not know the level of the intoxication and goes on with life as if nothing negative exists. Herein lies the deception, because the patient is sick, but the symptoms are not easy to identify. The patient progressively grows worse because the source of light, the Church, refuses to be assertive, giving the enemy access. That which the product highly esteems – religion – actually divides, bringing into bondage everyone that buys into this lie. The three branches of this government – legislative, judicial, and executive – are designed by the founders to work together, but because of the hidden toxins, they have inevitably become enemies.

These United States were not united when slavery was the issue. These United States remain divided when it comes to justice, equality, and equal opportunity for all of its citizens. The word "united" denotes agreement and harmony. How can agreement and harmony exist when there is widespread violation of the very laws promulgated by the product? The driving force that holds the nation together has to be unity, otherwise we are not the United States.

The inevitability of building on a flawed foundation is that the building will fall. Psalms 127:1 states, "Except the Lord builds the house, they labor in vain who build it; except the Lord keeps the city, the watchman wakes but in vain." Embracing the Words of the Manufacturer gives Him opportunity to build the house or the nation. The nation or city is only built by Him when those in the nation or city embrace His principles and know the Person of the principles. If He is not the Architect of the nation, every inch of the foundation is compromised, and all labor to build it is in vain. Furthermore, the nation or city is without protection in the form of Truth and light. If Truth and light have priority, then division and bitterness do not have access. Truth cannot produce bitterness and light cannot produce division.

The effect of deception is death for all those who reject Truth. Rejecting Truth empowers darkness and perpetuates selfishness. Self is invigorated when it is perpetuated. Self-centeredness is maximized when the words of the product take preference over the Words spoken by the Manufacturer. This separation from the Manufacturer is self-induced, based on the choices made by the product.

The Manufacturer is very protective of His glory. He will not give His glory to another (Isaiah 42:8). The word glory denotes the essence of a person or thing.[42] When the glory of the product rises above the glory of the Manufacturer, the result is idolatry. This brings severe consequences according to Ezekiel 23:49: "Thus your lewdness shall be recompensed upon you and you shall suffer the penalty for your sinful idolatry; and you shall know (understand and realize) that I am the Lord God."

A form of idolatry has crept into many aspects of society, the Church being the greatest culprit. The enemy knows that if he is able to plant idolatry in the Church, the authority and power of the Church will be compromised. The power of darkness uses religion to accomplish this. The objective is to create division within the Church by presenting a measure of truth surrounded by lies. The mandate for the Church is to produce light. Unfortunately, to a large degree, assimilation has been the result, and she has been incorporated into the world. Thus, the true nature of religion has to be exposed.

---

42   Hebrew-Greek Key Study Bible, p. 1708-1709

Christianity is not synonymous with religion, and this is part of the great challenge. The Manufacturer has no pleasure in religion. His pleasure is in relationship. The Son was not sent into the world to establish some form of religion, but to restore relationship. As long as religion remains dominant, relationship will never be established. The Fatherhood of God (the Manufacturer) is contingent on a personal relationship. I cannot call Him Father except through the revelation revealed by the Holy Spirit. He is not my father because I call Him Father. He is my Father because I have a personal relationship with Him, based on His plans and His purpose. His Son (Jesus) plays a vital role in establishing the reconnection to Him. John 1:12 says, "But to as many as did receive and welcome Him, He gave the authority (power, privilege, right) to become the children of God, that is, to those who believe in (adhere to, trust in, and rely on) His name."

The demand placed on the Church is to remind the nation of her commitment to what the Word says. Her commitment is to the Manufacturer. Again, the great commission of the Church is found in Mark 16:15-18, "And he said unto them, Go ye into all the world, and preach the gospel to every creature. He that believeth and is baptized shall be saved; but he that believeth not shall be damned. And these signs shall follow them that believe; In my name shall they cast out devils; they shall speak with new tongues; They shall take up serpents; and if they drink any deadly thing, it shall not hurt them; they shall lay hands on the sick, and they shall recover." Never once did Jesus say, "Go and preach religion."

Chapter Twelve

One Nation Under— Choose This Day Whom You Will Serve

Because an individual claims he is a Christian does not mean that his heart is connected to the Source (Jesus). Because a nation declares that it's "one nation under God" or that "in God we trust" does not mean it is connected to the Source. True connection is confirmed by believing in one's heart, and confessing with one's mouth that Jesus Christ is Lord. Romans 10: 9-10 tells us, "That if thou shalt confess with thy mouth the Lord Jesus, and shalt believe in thine heart that God hath raised him from the dead, thou shalt be saved. For with the heart man believeth unto righteousness; and with the mouth confession is made unto salvation." The trick of the enemy is to get the product to focus all of his attention on the words spoken, instead of on the commitment from the heart.

True believers recognize the value of what Jesus has provided and place a demand on themselves to be doers of the Word and not hearers only. A seed does not become a plant, nor does a plant bear fruit without going through a process. Productivity requires a change from a seed to a plant, from a plant to a plant with blooms, from a bloom to a fruit. In every seed there is a tree, and in every tree there is forest. A process is required to go from a seed to a tree and from a tree to a forest. A commitment to Jesus Christ goes beyond mere words. The lifestyles of people who openly confess their Christianity but lack integrity and accountability compromise the soundness of their convictions and project a flawed picture of what true Christianity is all about. They are like a seed that is destined to become a tree, but refuses to go through the process.

The motives that drive the product are his own desires and the erroneous belief that his ideas and opinions have parity with those of the Manufacturer. His beliefs allow him to choose whether or not to comply with the principles of the Manufacturer. In this lost state, he is unable to recognize his condition, and the very things he so highly esteems pushes him farther away from the Manufacturer.

When the product is driven by the Truth and the Word, he benefits. However, when the product is out of position and disconnected from the Manufacturer, his purpose for coming to Earth is forfeited and his destiny is not reached. He may appear successful in his own eyes, but not in the eyes of the Manufacturer. Disconnected from the Manufacturer, the product is without direction. Thus, his opinions are contaminated, his heart is corrupt, his eyes are blinded by sin, and he has lost the ability to live as opposed to merely existing. In this disconnected state, the product is controlled by his flesh and, because of this, the Holy Spirit is restrained and cannot perform what He was sent to Earth to do (John 14:26 and John 15:26).

Galatians 5:16-17 says, "But I say, walk and live [habitually] in the [Holy] Spirit [responsive to and controlled and guided by the Spirit]; then you will certainly not gratify the cravings and desires of the flesh (of human nature without God). For the desires of the flesh are opposed to the [Holy] Spirit, and the [desires of the] Spirit are opposed to the flesh [godless human nature]; for these are antagonistic to each other [continually withstanding and in conflict with each other], so that you are not free but are prevented from doing what you desire to do." The Holy Spirit is the support each believer needs. He reminds the believer of what the Manufacturer has said concerning the product.

When the Holy Spirit does not have access, the product draws from the one with whom he identifies, darkness and death. Genesis 1:26 reads, "Then God said, "Let us make man in our image, in our likeness, and let them rule over the fish of the sea and the birds of the air, over the livestock, over all the earth, and over all the creatures that move along the ground." Since the product is made in His image and likeness, he is designed to display His characteristics. When Adam fell, the product took on the image of likeness the power of darkness. John 8:44 says, "You are of your father, the devil, and it is your will to practice the lusts and gratify the desires [which are characteristic] of your father. He was a murderer from the beginning and does not stand in the truth, because there is no truth in him. When he speaks a falsehood, he speaks what is natural to him, for he is a liar [himself] and the father of lies and of all that is false."

The Bible says in Luke 19:10, "For the Son of Man came to seek and to save that which was lost." The product needs the presence of the Holy Spirit to lead him to the Son. When the product is disconnected from the Manufacturer, he cannot function according to the plan and purpose of the Manufacturer. Yet, in all of this, the product still has the ability to choose. Deuteronomy 30:19 says, "I call heaven and earth to witness this day against you that I have set before you life and death, the blessings and the curses; therefore choose life, that you and your descendants may live."

Life is choice-driven, and each person has to make the right choice. The product has the ability to make the right choice; however, discipline and commitment are required for the product to honor his own words and stand by his choice.

The Constitution, Bill of Rights and Declaration of Independence speak volumes regarding the words of the leaders. But, their words did not necessarily reflect what was in their hearts. The prophet expressed it this way in Isaiah 29:13: "The Lord says: These people come near to Me with their mouth and honor Me with their lips, but their hearts are far from me." There is a connection between the heart and the mouth. In an environment void of wisdom and light, what is said carries more weight than what is in the heart.

Changes do not occur on their own. Changes require planning and vision. Proverbs 29:18 states, "Where there is no vision [no redemptive revelation of God], the people perish: but he who keeps the law [of God, which includes that of man] blessed (happy, fortunate, and enviable) is he." A vision is a revelation from the Manufacturer; but, if the Manufacturer is not highest priority, revelation will not be forthcoming.

Since the product cannot change himself, nothing the product produces results in a lasting change; this requires a connection to the Source. Remember, the Source provides the way, the truth, and the life. The Source has a design for every aspect of the product, and nothing is hidden from Him. With the fall of Adam, the spirit of darkness has impacted everyone who has entered the world. However, one of the benefits of the Good News is Jesus removing the power of darkness, giving the product an opportunity to receive the only One who can bring about all the changes necessary to put him back on the right road.

Again, choosing the way of life of the Manufacturer requires discipline and total commitment. The product must accept all that Jesus has accomplished. This shifts the product's allegiance from darkness to light, from death to life. With this change, true love is introduced. 1 John 4:16 says, "And so we know and rely on the love God has for us. God is love. Whoever lives in love lives in God, and God in him." Verse 19 goes on: "We love Him because He first loved us." Love, through the eyes of darkness prevented the product from loving all; but, the love of the Manufacturer, through the finished work of Jesus Christ, equips the product to love even his enemies.

Love is a product of the Manufacturer. Love is the essence of who He is. Love enables the product to live above all circumstances, to love the unloved and the unlovely, and to abide in love. Love releases a spirit of forgiveness. Galatians 5:22-23 says, "But the fruit of the [Holy] Spirit [the work which His presence within accomplishes] is love, joy, (gladness), peace, patience (an even temper, forbearance), kindness, goodness (benevolence), faithfulness, gentleness (meekness, humility), self-control (self-restraint, continence). Against such things there is no law [that can bring a charge]." Unity is a product of love.

Obtaining total freedom is not within the ability of the product. The assumption has been that laws promulgated by the product address all of the challenges of the product, but the Creator of the product is the only One that knows how the product is designed to function. The product man is fearfully and wonderfully made (Psalm 139: 14). Therefore, the principles used by the product that are in opposition to those of the Manufacturer will cause the product to malfunction. When a higher value is placed on the product's opinions than on the principles of the Manufacturer, failure is inevitable.

One of the greatest liabilities of a democracy is freedom. The notion that the product can establish a system that gives total freedom is unfounded. Remember, the laws were established by flawed men, whose hearts were corrupted by pride, hatred, and racism. The principles of the Kingdom of Heaven are rooted and grounded in truth, while the laws of the kingdom of this world are rooted and ground in opinions, ideas, and the consensus of the majority. The opinion of the majority does not provide truth, nor does the opinion of the majority ensure compliance. For example, popular radio and television personalities of today, express their opinions- whether they are right, wrong or indifferent, they are just expressing their opinions, and not the Truth. However, they are protected by the same laws that gave them their ability to speak freely. They are mindful that these laws work to their advantage, because the laws were created by individuals with similar thoughts and objectives.

The fact remains that democracy is the product's idea, and not the Manufacturer's. For the Manufacturer to embrace democracy would mean

He has violated His own Word. Isaiah 42:8 says, "I am the Lord; that is My name! And My glory I will not give to another, nor My praise to graven images." He would have to lower His standard to embrace any system created by the product. By doing so, He would compromise His own Words. Hebrews 13:8 says, "Jesus Christ [the Messiah] is always the same, yesterday, today, and forever [to the ages]." The Bible is clear as to the credibility of His Word. He does not change, nor is He swayed by popular opinion.

The product is either a citizen of the Kingdom of Heaven or a citizen of the kingdom of this world. Dual citizenship is impossible, as this would suggest that the system of government in this nation is an extension of the system in the Kingdom of Heaven. Religious freedom has given this democracy a high level of credibility by selling the notion that it has the approval of the Manufacturer. The problem is that a kingdom is established upon religion is as inferior as all of the other kingdoms of the world. It is clear that religion has been exalted by the product, and herein lies the great challenge for the Church and the nation.

The Kingdom established by the Manufacturer is Superior to all kingdoms in the earth and the Heavens. It has dominion, rule and reign over every principality, high and low. With this revelation, one would wonder why the product would succumb to an inferior kingdom, when they can choose to reign and rule with the King of Kings and the Lord of Lords in the Kingdom of God. Thus, the product must choose whom he will serve, the "authority of the people", or the all-Knowing, All-Seeing, All-Powerful, God (Manufacturer). Joshua 24:15 says it the best, "And if it seems evil to you to serve the Lord, choose for yourself this day whom you will serve…"

Chapter Thirteen

The Call For Unity— Can We Walk Together?

The greatest challenge for this nation is in the arena of unity. Basic unity is essential in proclaiming the gospel. The unity between the Father and the Son was expressed by the Son in John 8:29: "And He Who Me is ever with Me: My Father has not left Me alone, for I always do what pleases Him." The Manufacturer is pleased when His Body functions as He designed it to function. Psalms 133:1 says, "Behold, how good and how pleasant it is for brethren to dwell together in unity." The best way to express the heart of the Manufacturer is through unity.

The Church has the mandate to instruct the believers and unbelievers about the principles of the Manufacturer, and His principles consist of total unity. Therefore, if there is one group that should be unified, it is the Church, the source of light to the world, salt to the earth, the Body of Christ. His Body, the Church, has been given keys to His Kingdom (Matthew 16:19). These keys are not based on ethnicity, wealth, or culture but on a personal relationship with the Manufacturer through the Son.

First Corinthians 12:27 says, "Now you [collectively] are Christ's body and [individually] you are members of it, each part severally and distinct [each with his own place and function]." The Bible also declares that the body is not one member, but many as Paul reminded the church in Ephesians 4:3-6: "Be eager and strive earnestly to guard and keep the harmony and oneness of [and produced by] the Spirit in the binding power and peace. [There is] one body and one Spirit just as there is also one hope [that belongs] to the calling you received. [There is] one Lord, one faith, one baptism. One God and Father of [us] all, Who is above all [Sovereign over all], pervading all and [living in us] all."

These scriptures are evidence that unity is the desire of the Father. He declared that He would build His church, and that the gates of hell could not prevail against it (Matthew 16:18).

Total unity requires the believer to abide in His Word and to allow His Word to abide in the believer's heart. Philippians 3:10 tell us, "[For my determined purpose is] that I may know Him [that I may progressively become more deeply and intimately acquainted with Him, perceiving and recognizing and understanding the wonders of His Person more strongly and more clearly], and that I may in that same way comet know the power flowing from His resurrection] which it exerts over believers], and that I may so share His sufferings as to be continually transformed [in spirit into His likeness even] this death." It should be the desire of every believer to know Him more each day. Such knowledge of Him produces unity.

As long as the product remains in the fallen state, unity is impossible. This state cannot be improved by either the product or by religion. Paul reveals in 1 Cor. 3:3, "For you are still [unspiritual, having the nature] of the flesh [under the control of ordinary impulses]. For as long as [there are] envying and jealousy and wrangling and factions among you, are you not unspiritual and of the flesh, behaving yourselves after a human standard and like mere (unchanged) men?" (This letter was written to Christians.) Because the Church has failed to produce light, darkness became the standard. Jealousy, resentment, and suspicion in the Church are traits driven by pride rooted and grounded in darkness, resulting in division. Disunity has opened the door to countless enemies working to undermine the foundation of Truth. It is unfortunate that, to a large degree, this objective has been achieved.

It is ironic that in the event of a national catastrophe, there is a tendency for the product to unite; but, this unity superficial and short-lived. The focus is merely external – unifying against outside threats –not against internal threats. When Pearl Harbor was attacked, and President Franklin Roosevelt called for unity, racism, sexism, segregation, greed, discrimination and injustice still lurked beneath the surface. Even the victims of injustice and inequality within the nation were united against the outside forces. This has been the pattern throughout this nation's history. It appears that as a nation, unity only rises to the forefront when external pressure is applied. It has never been a mandate of the nation, because after the catastrophe, the heart of the nation remains the same, divided. It has been back to business as usual. Blame is shifted and fingers are pointed, accusing one another.

Jesus gives us powerful wisdom on the consequences of division in Matthew 12:15: "And knowing their thoughts, He said to them, any kingdom that is divided against itself is being brought to desolation and laid waste, and no city or house divided against itself will last or continue to stand." Because division is a seed that produces a harvest of desolation, a nation divided cannot stand, no matter how prosperous it looks externally. While the harvest is not immediate, destruction and devastation will be the end result, unless a change occurs.

Unity requires a change in attitude, perception, and perspective, all of which will remain the same unless there is a change in allegiance. Jesus declared in John 14:6, "… I am the way and the truth and the life. No one comes to the Father except through Me." The way of Jesus Christ requires the product to comply with His principles. His principles require the product to love Him, as well as others. 1 John 4:7 says, "Dear friends, let us love another, for love comes from God. Everyone who loves has been born of God and knows God." Remember, the Church is His body, and each member is valuable.

His principles require the believers to unite because unity is an attribute of Him. In the prayer Jesus prayed for the believers in John 17:22-23, He expressed the value of unity: "I have given them the glory that you gave Me, that they may be one as we are one; I anthem and you in Me. May they be brought to complete unity to let the world know that You sent Me and have loved them even as You have loved Me." Unity requires the product to be in and remain in Him. This means leaders of the Church have a mandate from the Founder of the church to abide in Him.

The fact remains that the Church is the standard of unity. Again, it is a mandate from the Manufacturer. And, yet, the Church is the most segregated place in this nation on Sunday mornings. It is impossible to produce Light when the source of the Light is compromising truth. There is not a white church, a black church, an Asian church or a Hispanic church. There is only One Church, and that is The Church, and her founder is Jesus Christ. Jesus is coming back for His Church. His Church is comprised of many people of all ethnicities and nationalities unified and on one accord. When He returns He is not going to see black or white, male or female, but His Bride, the Body of Christ.

The Son became like the product in order to fulfill His assignment. Hebrews 2:14-15 says, "Since, therefore, [these His] children share in flesh and blood [in the physical nature of human beings], He [Himself] in a similar manner partook of the same [nature], that by [going through] death He might bring to nought and make of no affect him who had the power of death – that is, the devil – and also that He might deliver and completely set free all those who through the [haunting] fear of death were held in bondage throughout the whole course of their lives." Religion could not fulfill this assignment, because it required total unity between the Father, Son and Holy Spirit. The Father demanded it, the Son carried it out with His grace, and the Holy Spirit attracts the product to the Son.

Failing to walk together stems from deception being magnified, while Truth is being minimized. Thus, lies become the standard of thinking. Paul expressed it well in Romans 1:25: "They exchanged the truth of God for a lie, and worshipped and served created things rather than the Creator who is forever praised." The creature (the product) placed greater value on his own concepts, ideas, and opinions than on those of the Creator.

Greater emphasis has been placed on one's political persuasion than on the principles of the Manufacturer. Greater emphasis has also been placed on the opinions of the masses rather than on the principles of the Manufacturer. In the process, responsibilities have shifted. Wall Street is no longer held accountable for Main Street. Bankers, corporations, and politicians establish their own rules to give themselves the advantage. Each political party feeds off of and exploits the flaws of its opposing party, all while fostering disunity

What's a tragedy is that the Church's lack of leadership has contributed to division in the Church and in the nation. An even greater tragedy is that the Church does not recognize that she has contributed to the division. Separated from the Manufacturer, the product is in no position to provide the type of leadership that is needed because all of his strength, wisdom, knowledge, and understanding fall short. His thoughts are so inferior that they are foolish. Proverbs 21:2 tells us, "Every way of a man is right in his own eyes, but the Lord weighs and tries the heart."

As stated earlier, the product does not recognize his condition because he is disconnected from the Source. Just as the Trinity is in total unity, the Body of Christ should be in total unity. The nation cannot achieve unity when the kingdom of this world takes priority over the Kingdom of Heaven. This has propelled us into a downward spiral of great compromise, which affects how the product sees others, how they want others to see them, how they expect to be treated, how they deal with the Manufacturer, and how they respond to His commandments. Because some see themselves as the elite, the natural order of things dictates that division is as natural as summer and winter, spring and autumn. One group magnifies itself at the expense of the other, while the group on the other side buys into the devaluation and applauds the position of the other side. All the while both express their allegiance to the Manufacturer, but their hearts reflect what they have been taught by the kingdom of this world. As a result, opinions take preference over Truth, light, and righteousness.

The reason for disunity in the Church, as well as the nation is that more emphasis is placed on the flag and the nation's foundational documents than on the Word and Truth. Many leaders in the Church have wrapped themselves in the flag and the words of these documents, placing greater value on the founders than on the Son. The founders could not provide access to the Father (Manufacturer). They were merely the sinful descendants of Adam and were not above reproach. They did not have the corner on Truth, for all have sinned (Romans 3:23). The notion that the Holy Manufacturer would lower His standards to appease the product is beyond reason. His means of dealing with the sin of the product was to send His Son to become sin so that the product could be reconnected to the Manufacturer, because of His love for all humanity. Yet, despite knowledge of His Word, the founders took a position of opposition by designating certain ethnic groups as leaders and others as subservient.

This ungodly position has opened the door to division, deception, racism, sexism, and the elevation of religion. As a result, each generation continues to dismantle all traits of unity and today, unity is the exception and not the norm. Unity is not within the ability of the product without direct intervention from the Manufacturer. This intervention has been provided in the presence of the Lord Jesus Christ, but He must become priority in every life.

When pure unity, as portrayed by the Holy Trinity, takes place over religion, it will overcome all forms of hatred, prejudices, racism, bigotry, pride, greed and division. Pure unity allows a nation made up of individuals to walk together as one, because the focus is not on the "authority of the people," but the will of the Manufacturer.

Final Thoughts

Throughout history, religion has sought to represent Him (God), but has rejected His Word, His truth, His way, and His life. Religion creates a picture of the Manufacturer (God) as the Supreme Being, but fails to convey His desire for each product to release their potential, fulfill their purpose, and maximize their relationship with the Manufacturer.

Religion has accomplished its mission when Jesus Christ is reduced to the level of just another prophet. The lie that He is just another prophet causes the finished work of Jesus Christ to be looked upon as insignificant and irrelevant.

The Manufacturer created the product to enjoy the relationship of unity as depicted in the Holy Trinity. Thus, if a nation, or people, is to succeed, this has to be the goal. It is the only hope for a nation to flourish. Unity cannot and will not exist until the Manufacturer takes His rightful place on the throne in the heart of the nation and in the hearts of the people.

The question in the introduction was: When have we walked together? Now the focus should be: Isn't it time we walked together? After all, our currency depicts "In God We Trust" and our Pledge of Allegiance claims that we are, "one nation under God."

God Bless

Works Cited

Ferguson, Wallace K. and Geoffrey Brown. *A Survey of European Civilization*, Fourth Edition. Boston: Houston Mifflin Company, 1969.

Roark, James L., Michael P. Johnson, Patricia Cline Cohen, Sarah Stage, Alan Lawson and Susan M. Hartman. *The American Promise: A History of the United States: Volume I to 1877*, Boston-New York: Bedford/ St. Martins', 2003.

Spielvogel, Jackson J. *Western Civilization: Volume II, Since 1550*. St. Paul-New York-Los Angeles-San Francisco: West Publishing Company, 1991.

Divine, Robert A., T. H. Breen, George M. Frederickson and R. Hal Williams. *America Past and Present: Volume I to 1877*. Glenview Illinois: Scott Foreman and Company, 1984.

Franklin, John Hope and Alfred A. Moss Jr. *From Slavery to Freedom: A History of American Negros*, Sixth Edition. New York: McGraw-Hill, Inc., 1988

Boyer, Paul S., Clifford E. Clark Jr., Jospheh F. Kett, Neal Salisbury, Harvard Sitkoff and Nancy Woloch. *The Enduring Vision: A History of the American People: Volume One to 1877*, Second Edition. Lexington, Massachusetts: D.C. heath and Company, 1993

Carter, Dan T. *The Politics of Rage: George Wallace, the Origins of the New Conservatism, and the Transformation of American Politics*. New York: Simon & Schuster, 1995

Chambers, Mortimer, Raymond Grew, David Herlihy, Theodore K. Rabb and Isser Woloch. *The Western Experience: Volume I to 1715*, Fourth Edition. New York: Alfred A. Knopf, Inc., 1987

Class Structure. Class. The Free Online Dictionary & Encyclopedia (TFODE). (Wikipedia). <http://enc.tfode.com/social-cast#Europe>. "1, 2, 4-6, 8, 115." Retrieved July 2012

www.ingramcontent.com/pod-product-compliance
Lightning Source LLC
Chambersburg PA
CBHW050558300426
44112CB00013B/1979